AMERICA'S NEW "WOLF"

by Gene Letourneau

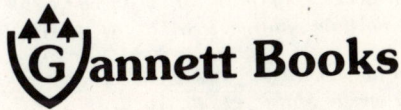

Guy Gannett Publishing Co.
Portland/Maine

Copyright © Gene Letourneau and Guy Gannett Publishing Co., 1984.

All rights reserved. No part of this work may be reproduced or transmitted in any form by any means, electronic or mechanical, including photocopying and recording, or by any information storage or retrieval system, without permission in writing from the publisher, except by a reviewer who may quote brief passages for a review.

Published by Gannett Books, Guy Gannett Publishing Co.,
390 Congress Street, Portland, Maine, USA, 04101, April, 1984.

First edition printed in the United States of America by
Gannett Graphics, Augusta, Maine, 04330, April, 1984.

Library of Congress Catalog Card # 82-80949.
ISBN # 0-930096-34-7.

Table of Contents

My First Sightings	1
Scientists Focus on The Mystery Animal	23
Feeding Habits	35
How Predators Kill	45
What About Winter Deer Kills	61
To Control or Not Control	67
How Dangerous To People	85
The People Speak	93
Conclusion	105

To All My Family

AMERICA'S NEW "WOLF"

by Gene Letourneau

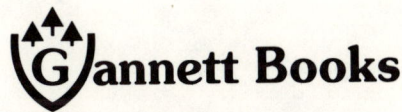
Gannett Books

Guy Gannett Publishing Co.
Portland/Maine

FOREWORD

No animal in the colorful history of Maine wildlife has created as much confusion and controversy as the one most commonly identified as the northeastern coyote and known scientifically as *Canis Latrans*. While the animal first made its presence known in the state in the early 1950s, it could well have been around before then. There is no evidence, however, that such an animal is native to Maine.

The University of Maine at Orono Wildlife Research Unit has identified it as a northeastern coyote. But wildlife experts continue to disagree about its true identity, describing it as a brush wolf, a mixture of coyote and red wolf and a combination of coyote, wolf and domestic dog. Weighing an average of more than thirty pounds — about twice the size of the western coyote — it might more properly be described as the wild, mystery mongrel of the century.

Many experienced outdoorsmen believe the increased presence of the animal in more and more parts of Maine from 1960 through 1983 was one of the prime causes of a steady decline in deer populations. The sentiment, however, is hardly shared by scientific and technical wildlife researchers who attributed the decline to a combination of more extensive lumbering operations, several harsh winters and increased hunting pressure.

To date, the debate probably has done more to confuse the issue than to clarify it. The exchange has been characterized by emotional arguments based on theory and general observations rather than hard data. But steps are being taken to increase the information base. As this book was being written, the University's Wildlife Research Unit was in the process of researching the animal's relation to land fur-bearers. The project included capturing coyote puppies, attaching radio transmitting collars to them and turning them loose in areas where adult coyotes were suspected of playing a significant role in the decimation of the deer herd.

Meanwhile, coyote control programs are under way on both the state and federal levels. The U.S. Fish and Wildlife Service's program is aimed at protecting livestock, principally sheep; the Maine program is designed to protect deer in areas where coyote predation was taking place.

The key question, at least in Maine, appears to be whether the northeastern coyote should be accepted as part of the ecosystem and given *carte blanche* or have its population controlled.

The scientific branch of the Maine Department of Inland Fisheries and Wildlife believes the animal is here to stay and that little can be done to control its population and range. The nonscientific branch believes control is possible on a regional basis and should take place to protect livestock and white-tailed deer. Several states have instituted control programs, but the impasse in Maine — where the faction in favor of controls recently won a few minor concessions — could continue for years to come.

My First Sightings

January 9, 1962, was a cold windy day in the unbroken wilderness expanse between the two international highways that run from Maine to Quebec. In the company of Arthur "Tibbie" Thibodeau and a brace of hounds, I was checking my side of the Spencer Lake road for signs of bobcat. The road was part of a 50-mile network of highways and hauling roads that extended from Parlin Pond to Coburn Gore, north of Eustis. It cut through one of the state's best habitats for bobcat and deer.

A powerful, athletic man, Tibbie had taken early retirement from his job as police chief of Waterville, my howntown. He augmented his retirement income by guiding fishing parties in the spring and summer but reserved the remainder of the year for his own enjoyment of outdoor sports. One of his favorites was bobcat hunting.

Our relationship dated back to high school in the early 1920s. It grew closer with the years, interrupted only when he went off to Shenandoah (Virginia) Military Academy — where he was a star football player — while I attended Thomas Business College in Waterville.

We had covered about eight miles that January 9th when we came upon an unplowed section of the road. The next four miles to Spencer Lake being the best area for bobcats, we parked the jeep and donned snowshoes, determined to cover the country thoroughly.

At the time, deer yarded in an area northeast of Spencer Lake, and it was not uncommon to see herds of up to 20 when the snow became deep. During some of the winters of the late 1950s and early 1960s, we estimated as many as 100 deer would gather in the yard to spend the winters. They would attract what was then their only serious predator, the bobcat. Finding a track of the wild feline consequently was rather simple.

Tibbie was breaking a path in the ten inches of snow while I trudged several yards behind him with Jack, a Walker hound we had decided to use that day, at heel.

Spencer Lake country near Jackman was among the first to harbor packs of northeastern coyotes. This view was taken from Bear Hill, looking west, on the original road to Spencer Lake, from Route 201 at Lake Parlin.

As we approached the deer yard I noticed Tibbie stop suddenly and look down. That usually meant he had spotted a bobcat track. I had not quite reached him when he turned toward me, shook his head, and declared, "These must be the tracks of the largest foxes I've ever seen or else there are stray hounds in the county."

Securing Jack to a nearby tree, I joined Tibbie in checking the unusual dog-like tracks. From what we could deduce there were four animals traveling together, fanning a deer trail.

Less than a quarter of a mile from the road we came upon the remains of an adult deer. It had been ripped apart, unlike the work of bobcats, and the ribs were missing, evidence that powerful jaws had been involved in this drama.

A few days later I returned to the scene with another longtime bobcat hunting friend, Harold McCaslin of Winslow, to take pictures.

This is what remained of a deer killed in December, 1972, by northeastern coyotes at Spencer Lake, Jackman area. Note how ribs had been cracked and some eaten, something no other known Maine predator would do. Harold McGaslin of Winslow, my bobcat hunting companion, was with me.

The incident encouraged me to investigate many subsequent reports of coyote sightings throughout the state. My observations have led me to form some strong opinions about the most controversial issue I have encountered in 53 years of covering Maine's outdoors: Should the mysterious animal be artificially managed to minimize its impact on the deer herd?

My first "true" wolf sighting occurred in Alaska in 1947 when I was a member of a pioneer group of outdoor writers making the first organized fishing-hunting-observation trip to what would become the 49th state.

Riding on the Alaskan highway from Dawson City to Otter Lake in company of the late Joe Brooks, whose fishing books are among the best ever written, and Viv Gray, then outdoors editor of the Cleveland Plain Dealer, we came upon four wolves devouring a big bull moose in a ditch alongside the road. The wolves left reluctantly when the driver of our car, an Army officer, got out and fired at them with a pistol. He then put the moose out of his misery, noting that there were still signs of life in the huge animal.

Some twenty years later, flying over tundra in Labrador while on a fishing trip, pilot Roger Holt of Greenville pointed out to me three "wolf-like" animals following a caribou migration route, a well-defined hoof-padded trail. Like the animals I had seen in Alaska, they seemed larger than the first northeastern coyotes I examined in Maine. But not much.

It's impossible to know when coyotes first roamed the state, but my first sighting of wolf-like creatures occurred in the winter of 1946. I have every reason to believe they were the same species that can now be found in every corner of Maine.

That initial observation was made at an outpost camp that my publisher, Guy P. Gannett, had built five years earlier to provide him and his guests added access to a wilderness teeming with fish and wildlife. The location was Chemquasabamticook Lake, also known as Ross Lake, the most isolated body of water in northwestern Maine. It could be reached only by plane or by canoeing 16 miles up the outlet stream from Clayton Lake.

I watched the animals as they trotted on the east shore of Ross Lake about a half-mile from the camp. Although I had adequate binoculars, I was unable to determine accurately their principal characteristics, but I was sure they were larger than an adult fox or a western coyote and more grayish and black-furred than the latter.

Within a few years I began to receive word of "wolf" and "mountain lion" sightings in the upper St. John and Allagash regions. The observers included Lionel Caron, born and brought up at Seven Islands on the St. John, and Carl Holden and his wife Margo, who resided at Clayton Lake while he was woods supervisor for International Paper Company.

Caron and the Holdens were sure that even in the late 1960s the area was well populated with the animal technically identified as the northeastern coyote.

On November 16, 1972 I examined two live coyotes that trappers John Wagg and Bill Lane had caught at Spencer Lake. Although they were primarily interested in beavers and bobcats, I had asked them to set for the "strange animal" in the area where its tracks now outnumbered those of bobcats.

The two animals, obviously spring pups, weighed less than 30 pounds each. But they had the tawny coats, the light bar of red on their ear tips, and the black rear saddle that would be noted on others examined later.

A suggestion that the state subsidize Wagg and Lane that spring so they could concentrate on stemming the increase of coyotes in the area went unheeded.

My first close field sighting of coyotes occurred in May, 1974. I was walking a trail in the Ten Thousand Acre Tract, east of Route 201 between West Forks and Parlin Pond. Cross-country the area is about 15 miles from Spencer Lake. My son-in-law, Sidney Dupont, was with me. The wind was blowing hard in our favor when we came upon a wolf-like animal standing still in the trail and looking the opposite direction from which we were approaching. I estimated its weight at close to fifty pounds, although Sid thought it would weigh a great deal more.

Because the incident occurred late in the spring, the animal's fur had faded to a tawny gray. It was streaked with black on the back and the top of the tail, and had a reddish line at the shoulders. The abrupt muzzle and pointed ears suggested a wolf. The animal did not seem alarmed, probably because he did not wind us. He trotted off the trail and we continued walking.

Less than 50 yards farther on I spotted two more of the creatures on the trail. They were smaller and had come onto the path behind a deer. Tracks of the deer, apparently a yearling, and of the two coyotes continued a short distance before veering off — all in the same direction.

Bud Wagg and Walter Lane were among the first trappers to catch a coyote when they showed up in the Spencer Lake (Jackman) region. In picture above they approach the number one coyote they trapped, on November 16, 1972.

With no snow, tracking the animals was out of the question. There could be little doubt, however, that the coyotes were following the deer, one of the very few still left in a part of Maine where, in several previous winters, I had found a number of deer kills by coyotes.

Two months earlier, I was driving on Route 150 between Skowhegan and Athens when I saw a large coyote standing in the center of the highway. While my plan for the day was to find a bobcat track for my hounds to unravel, I stopped and attempted a stalk on the coyote, which loped into the woods as I approached it.

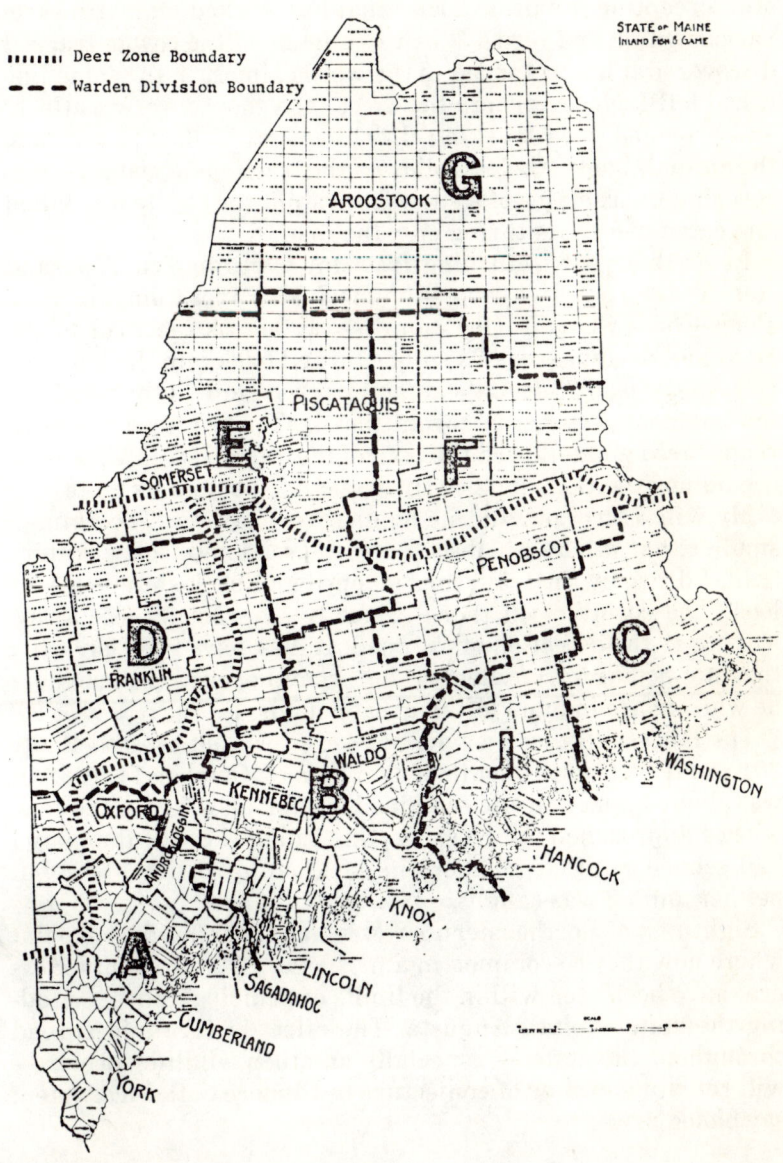

The above map shows deer zone and warden division boundaries as noted. The author's first discovery of deer predation by coyotes was in Division E, Somerset County. It is generally agreed that the migration of coyotes in Maine has been west to east or from left to right of the above map. (Courtesy Fisheries-Wildlife Department.)

A 12-gauge in hand, I entered the woods at an angle in hopes of intercepting my prey, a ruse that has worked many times on various game and birds. When I came upon the coyote track, I discovered it had returned to the woods almost in the same line it had left them. Although the three-inch snow cover was fluffy and provided good tracking, I doubted my ability to overtake the animal. I nevertheless followed the track some distance, discovering the remains of a snowshoe rabbit the coyote had killed and eaten before venturing onto the road.

Later that year, returning from my camp in Ten Thousand Acre Tract, I saw two coyotes on the Scott Paper Company road along Chase Stream. One ran directly across the road to the right and disappeared. The other turned back into the left side. I drove the jeep 75 feet ahead and parked close to the woods. A few moments later, the coyote that had not crossed the road reappeared and followed the trail of the other. If it saw the jeep, it paid no attention, apparently determined to join its mate.

My wife Lou was with me on another sighting. The animal, smaller than others I had seen, left the road and took a skidder trail. I drove by the trail, then stopped and backed up to take a look. The coyote stood there perfectly still, not 50 feet away, looking in the direction of the road. It may have been curiosity that stopped him from fleeing, but when I opened the jeep door he whirled around and left in great bounds.

The largest coyotes I have seen were two that crossed Route 201 about three miles south of Jackman on October 14, 1982. It was about 4 p.m. and one remained within a few feet of the road when I approached the crossing. One had darker fur than any I had seen. I notified trappers in Jackman of the sighting but neither animal was caught.

Sightings of northeastern coyotes have increased to a point where now they're common in almost every Maine county. Several have been seen within the limits of principal cities, including the state capital, Augusta. The effect of its rapid spread throughout the state — especially on other wildlife species — will remain a matter of conjecture until more data is collected, say biologists.

What Is It?
Where Did It Come From?

Knowledgeable outdoorsmen have reported sightings of large German Shepherd dogs, wolves, cougars and coyotes in the Maine woods for the past several decades. If nothing else, the conflicting reports are a good indicator of the uncertainty that has accompanied the emergence of the coyote, an uncertainty that persists even today.

A 1939 paper by Clarence M. Aldous of the Bureau of Biological Survey, University of Maine, Orono documents the early confusion concerning the true identity of the animals. Published in the *Journal of Mammology* under the title of "Coyotes in Maine," it notes that the wolf, an animal native to the state, had all but disappeared several years before the coyote's presence became known.

"Before 1900, wolves were native to the state of Maine," Aldous wrote, "but since that date no authentic records are known of their being seen. A supposed wolf, shot in November, 1936, was brought to my attention but this animal proved to be a coyote of the plains variety and not a wolf as had been reported and widely publicized. . . . Unlike the wolf, the coyote was never native in Maine."

Ross McKenney, who later became director of Dartmouth's outdoor program, shot the animal in the northeast corner of Argyle Township in Penobscot County. He thought he had bagged a male wolf, but a closer inspection proved otherwise. Wrote Aldous: "On November 11, Dr. W. B. Bell, Dr. H. H. T. Jackson, Leo K. Couch, all of the Biological Survey, and I examined this skin. All were in accord that the animal was a coyote, very closely resembling the plains species.

"In January, 1937, Percy Storer trapped what appeared to be another of these animals, an adult male. It was taken in Edinburg Township, about four miles north of the place where McKenney had made his capture. I saw this animal and identified it as a coyote.

"The following weight and measurements were taken: weight, 32 pounds; total length, 51 inches; tail, 13¼ inches; hind foot, 7½ inches; ear, from notch, 4¼ inches."

Trappers Maurice Stevens, Leo Ross and Clyde Hichburn contributed 12 specimens to Aldous in 1938. Ten of them, including two pups, were taken in Edinburg Township. Two males taken by Stevens were somewhat different and their skulls were sent to the Bureau of Biological Survey and examined by Major E. A. Goldman, who reported:

"These two are clearly not full-blooded coyotes although the skulls resemble coyote skulls in a number of respects ... and while I can say positively that the skulls are not from full-blooded coyotes, they might possibly be of dogs or more likely the result of a coyote-dog cross. Both of these are adults and are larger and heavier than coyotes, with shorter canine teeth and they differ in a number of other details."

Of the animals taken in the Edinburg area Aldous wrote: "It is interesting to note that all these captures were made in a very localized area, seven within a radius of a mile. Just how these animals came to this restricted area is still a mystery, but it is highly probable that some individual procured one or more of them for pets from the western part of the country and then, either by accident or by deliberate intent, released them."

In December, 1961, while on my way to The Forks, I noticed a wolf-like animal hanging at the home of Oliver Adams. After learning it had been struck by a pulp truck, I suggested he turn it over to the University of Maine Cooperative Wildlife Research Unit for examination. It was the first such animal I knew of to be killed in Somerset County.

Howard L. Mendall, leader of the research unit at the time, reported a few weeks later that it had been identified as a northeastern coyote *(Canis latrans thamnos)* by Dr. Richard H. Manville, director, Bird and Mammal Laboratories, Bureau of Sports Fisheries and Wildlife, Washington, D.C.

During the previous winter, several canid skulls and a pelt had been sent to the same laboratories by Kenneth W. Hodgdon, then assistant chief of Maine's Game Division. The report from Thomas D. Burleigh, assistant director of the Wildlife Research branch of the Bureau of Sports Fisheries and Wildlife, helped explain why the animals defied easy identification.

Noting that it is generally possible to distinguish between pure dogs and pure coyotes, Burleigh pointed out that the two species "freely interbreed in the wild, and may produce offspring that resemble either parent or any degree of intermediate. The coyote has been moving eastward for many years and has interbred with feral or domestic dogs in the process, so that today we are dealing with dogs and coyotes that have interbred for many years and whose offspring have been interbreeding and may exhibit any degree of the mixture of characters.

"In the case of the specimens you sent to us, we are dealing with such hybrid animals. Cranially they are similar to coyotes of the sub-species thamnos. The diagnostic characters on the

Glenn H. Manuel, Maine's commissioner of Fisheries-Wildlife.

skulls are predominantly coyote. The hide, however, shows that at least this one animal was mixed with dog and makes us suspicious of the other two.

"Of the hundreds of coyote skins in our reference collections, none of them resembles the very dark hide you sent us and nobody here has ever seen a pure coyote so marked. We would identify this animal as a dog-coyote hybrid, showing marked coyote characteristics in the cranium and dog characteristics in the pelage. In layman's language, the skull was coyote-like, the fur, dog-like."

It's reasonable to expect the average hunter, trapper and out doorsman to disagree about the true identity of an animal that appears so suddenly in an entirely new environment. On the other hand, you would expect the scientific experts to be in agreement on the matter. But that is not the case. The animal had more aliases than a convicted felon. Among them: northeastern coyote, brush wolf, timber wolf, red wolf-coyote cross, domestic dog-wolf cross, dog-coyote cross, and "New Wolf."

Voit B. Richens, assistant professor of Wildlife Resources for many years, holds to his earliest findings. Richens in 1972 examined a "wild wolf-like or coyote-like" animal shot in Millinocket and identified it as an eastern coyote *(Canis Latrans var)*. His conclusions were based on pelt coloring, appendage characteristics, tooth size, and skull and body measurements. The specimen was a mature male weighing 51 pounds, with a body length of 45 inches, the largest examined in Maine up to that time.

Richens in 1961 also had examined and identified as a northeastern coyote the animal killed by a pulp truck in Somerset County. It weighed 38 pounds, but since then many have been considerably larger. The largest, a 78-pounder trapped by Terry Richardson of Gorham in the Kennebago region, was confirmed by Commissioner Glenn Manuel of the Fish and Wildlife Department.

Opinions regarding the identity of the animal differed widely as more were killed and trapped. Three taken in eastern Quebec, not far from the Maine border, in the winter of 1961 were described as timber wolf-coyote crosses by Canadian authorities who examined them.

During the same winter, Aimé LeCours, for over 50 years a trapper based at Skinner, 30 miles west of Jackman, told me he had seen three "wolf-like" animals on a flowage he had set for

Pack on back, Aime LeCours returns to his Skinner camp after trek with his Cocker Spaniel dog. LeCours was the first to report presence of unusually large, wolflike animals in that part of Maine which is about 14 miles west of Jackman.

beavers. When he failed to see them or their tracks again, LeCours concluded that they were the same animals trapped in Quebec.

Among the "experts" who first questioned the true identity of the animals was Dr. Raymond P. Coppinger, an associate professor of biology at Hampshire College, Amherst, Massachusetts. Coppinger coined the name "new wolf" for the animal and contended it had evolved in the forests of New England as an "adaptation" to the environment.

Coppinger is typical of those who believe the animal is a welcome addition to the wildlife of the northeast. He contends the animal is an "opportunistic predator" — that it does not expend energy unless other methods of finding food fail.

Coppinger contends the animal is unique to the area and shouldn't be strictly equated with the western coyote. One of the reasons, he adds, is that the tissue of the New England new wolf is more wolf than coyote.

William Bossert, a biologist in Harvard University's division of engineering and applied physics, presents another theory concerning the invasion of the animal, and its size. Bossert contends the animals could have hybridized with wolves in southern Ontario, or that the coyotes, not having competition in their new environment, have envolved rapidly to be more wolf-like.

Bossert has done a series of detailed field studies on the skulls of wolves, coyotes, and dogs in collaboration with Barbara Lawrence of Harvard's Museum of Comparative Zoology. She is considered a leading expert on the domestic dog. Bossert has said there is no evidence the animal has been hybridizing with dogs, a deduction based on the results of skull measurements made by Harvard researchers.

I kept in close touch with developments concerning the new canid in Maine, writing frequent columns about them. On December 9, 1974, Henry Hilton, then a research assistant with the Maine Game Division who later transferred to Program Development and Coordination, and now is in charge of Nuisance Animal Control, wrote me concerning several columns. Following are some of his comments:

"The name 'new wolf' was conferred upon the coyote by Dr. Coppinger who wrote an article for Massachusetts Wildlife entitled 'Meet the New Wolf.' When he met with us recently, Dr. Coppinger disclaimed responsibility for that title. While he admits that the animal basically is a coyote, he still uses the

Henry Hilton, coordinator of Maine's Nuisance Animal Control Program.

name because, he says, it saves a lot of time. Dr. Coppinger stands alone. Calling the coyote a 'new wolf' is analogous to calling a large bobcat a new lynx.

"The coyotes in Maine are very similar to the coyotes I looked at recently at the Denver Wildlife Research Center in Colorado. The pelt coloration and patterns are conformation — all somewhat variable — are strikingly similar. The difference is in size, 25 pounds for Texas coyotes compared to 35-40 pounds for Maine coyotes. There are also differences in skull measurements which we are still trying to evaluate. But the animal is not a wolf, old or new.

"The number of large coyotes reported is interesting. This fall

(1974) four animals were reputed to weigh over 60 pounds but when they were sent to the Wildlife Unit I found the heaviest to weigh 43.5 pounds and the others from 26 to 35 pounds.

"There are many dogs running wild, two of which you pictured from Allen's Mills and called coyotes. And there are, undoubtedly, some coyote-dog crosses, but these are hard to identify because a cross between coyotes and dogs looks like the dog, not the coyote.

"You have referred to studies by other states and observations by Maine trappers but put little emphasis on research done in Maine on coyotes. Since 1968, over 130 coyotes have been examined at the Maine Wildlife Research Unit. A summary of information through 1973 is published by Dr. Voit Richens and Roy Hugie in the Journal of Wildlife Management.

"Other northeastern states have good material on coyotes. The New York Conservationist ran two excellent articles on food habits, distribution, range, habits and behavioral characteristics. All of these articles are more pertinent than coyote studies done in Arizona."

In a paper published in 1978 by Academic Press, Inc., Hilton wrote in part:

"Individual skulls from New Hampshire, Maine and Quebec vary from being coyote-like in narrowness of the rostrum, in inflation and elevation of the braincase, and in relative size of teeth, to being uncoyote-like in the shorter rostrum, in the elevated frontals and in the disproportionate dental characters.

"Maine coyote skulls averaged six and eleven percent larger than those of western coyotes in total length and breadth, respectively.

"Unlike western coyotes, the Maine skulls invariably lacked the round protuberance of the occiput and the accessory cuspion. Like wolves, the braincase was positioned low, the post-orbital region was well separated from the anterior constriction of the braincase and the frontal shield was moderately elevated.

"In a recent application of the discriminant function technique, I found that of the available canid skulls collected in Maine from 1968 to 1976, all but three were positioned intermediate to coyotes and wolves in the same general range as the New Hampshire animals. The remainder were unmistakingly dogs and no coyote-dog hybrids were recognized."

Earl H. Smith of Northland Wolf Colony, Wells, Maine, threw new light on the possible true strain of the new animal in a letter protesting my reference to the new "predator" as a threat to the Maine deer herd.

The letter was lengthy and extolled the virtues of the wolf in the ecosystem. But the part of it referring to his father, Gordon Smith, who has written about the "Great Plains Wolf — *Canis lupus nubiluser*," caught my eye. Smith said his father, then a young man in the 1930s, helped catch and ship east large numbers of coyotes, M.V. Red wolves and remnant crosses of lycanon and nubilus wolves. "Eastern coyote? New Wolf? We will let the know-it-all biologists fight over (true identification) while I laugh so hard I cry . . . ," Smith wrote.

Smith also suggested that I watch for reports of new wolves in Western Iowa, Northern Illinois and several other places. According to him, there are no so-called timber wolves in Maine.

Still another version of the evolution and migration routes of the Northeastern Coyotes is noted in a study made at Pennsylvania State University. It indicates the animal may be a cross between the Algonquin wolf and the common Western Coyote.

Helen McGinnis, wildlife biologist at Penn State, contends the canid now in Maine migrated eastward by crossing frozen rivers of the midwest into southern Ontario and from there into Quebec, New York, New England and New Brunswick.

Her study also indicated that during the migrations, the coyotes would occasionally breed with wolves and dogs as well as other coyotes. The findings help explain the conflicting results of laboratory examinations of the animals.

Frank Woolner, an author of several outdoors books, differs with Smith's evaluation of the new animal's place in today's ecosystem, but Woolner has long contended that it has genes of the red wolf. He believes the animal has become a serious threat to whitetail deer.

Woolner, bases his findings on examinations of a number of "coyotes" taken in his native Massachusetts. The reddish fur around the ears and the top of the head, he says, are unmistakable features of the rare red wolf.

In 1974, the Minnesota Department of Natural Resources succeeded in having the "timber wolf" declassified as an endangered species. Robert L. Herbst, Minnesota's commissioner of Natural Resources, noted at the time that the sustained annual harvest under the bounty system, the continued need for predator control outside of the main wolf range and the general

Warden Linwood Folsom is shown with 80-pound animal identified by a Washington laboratory as a female timber wolf. It was killed in Cherryfield in November, 1953 and added to the confusion developing over the true identity of a new predatory animal in Maine. (Photo courtesy Bangor Daily News.)

timber wolf population increase in Minnesota since 1965 indicate a thriving wolf population.

The description of the timber wolf by Minnesota biological experts certainly fits some of the "coyotes" I have examined in Maine:

"The timber wolf (or gray wolf) is a wild dog-like animal that usually lives in packs of two to twelve. It often kills large animals such as deer and moose for food.

Marcelle LaRochelle of St. Prosper, P.Q. with 50 pound "timber wolf" he bagged in the fall of 1981 in northern Quebec while on a moose hunt. It looked much like the same animal bagged in Cherryfield in 1953. LaRochelle, a veteran outdoorsman who has trapped a number of northeastern coyotes on the Quebec—Maine border, has noted a difference between them and the wolf he shot.

John Guptill chats with author while displaying a picture of the largest coyote he caught during an outbreak in Waldo County. It weighed 48 pounds, its true identity questioned.

"Timber wolves normally are gray in color, darker on the back and often have a brown or reddish coat during the summer. Lighter or darker colored animals are seen occasionally but cream-colored or black wolves are seen only rarely.

"Home range of wolf packs usually varies from 50 to 100 square miles. The timber wolf is capable of running several miles at speeds of 30 to 35 miles per hour and will often cover 40 miles in a single night.

"Minnesota's timber wolves stand 28 to 30 inches high at the shoulder. Adult females reach weights of 45 to 85 pounds and adult males weigh from 65 to 90 pounds. Pups often reach adult weight before they are a year old."

The animal very much in the Maine limelight today has not reached average size and weight of the typical Minnesota timber wolf, but some may be getting there. Experts and practical wildlife buffs will continue to argue over its true identity, but one thing is certain: Maine has a brand new animal, lauded and cursed as no other.

Scientists Focus on The Mystery Animal

Although the Maine Fisheries-Wildlife Department over the years had received numerous reports of deer kills indicating a rapidly expanding coyote population, it was not until the winter of 1973 that a study took place.

As early as 1962, I had reported the presence of a new predator in the Spencer Lake region, west of Jackman, and written articles expressing concern that the coyote would become a menace to deer, certainly in all areas north and west of the Appalachian Trail, unless some means of control was undertaken.

However, neither Maynard F. Marsh, then commissioner of Fisheries and Wildlife, nor Robert Boettger and Chester Banasiak of the Game Division believed the deer-coyote situation was becoming serious. The response of state biologists typically was the coyotes "are here and we must live with them."

It was Francis J. Gramlich, Maine agent for the U.S. Fish and Wildlife Service, who helped promote and finance the first coyote study in the Spencer Lake area. The Maine Fisheries-Wildlife Department and the federal service shared expenses, although the eventual cost never was disclosed.

While several experienced woodsmen and trappers were available and willing to cooperate in the study, none was asked to. Instead, three Colby College students were selected as part of the college's January, 1973, program of Independent Study. They were David Hoitt of Putney, Vermont, Christopher Metcalf of Falmouth, Mass., and Joel Ossoff of Oneida, Tennessee. Although all were energetic young men, they lacked Maine woods experience and wildlife tracking lore.

In the preface of their eventual report, the students noted that the "advice and assistance of District Warden Supervisor Vernon Moulton and wardens Glenn Feeney and Carroll Goodwin were essential in conducting the study. The location of coyote tracks and deer kills were frequently provided by the above."

The purpose of the study was twofold: "To provide a learning experience for the participating students and to glean some information on the behavior of the Maine coyote. Of special interest were the feeding habits and diet of the coyote since it is felt by some that this predator may be having an adverse effect on deer populations..."

Except for one four-day backpack trip, the Colby students collected their data by making daily trips from their quarters in Jackman. The selected area included portions of Long Pond and Attean and Spencer lakes as bounded on U.S. Geological maps.

On several occasions, especially in areas close to Jackman, domestic dogs hampered tracking efforts, forcing the students to restrict their study to areas far removed from domestic dog populations.

The survey report noted under field observations that "as might be expected, no visual sightings of coyotes were made and, therefore, all observations of behavior were obtained by studying tracks. The short time period available for the study allowed, even under ideal conditions, for only a very brief and inadequate study."

The report also pointed out that "no specific attempt was made to estimate numbers of coyotes present in the areas studied... First, it seems very possible that the presence of domestic dogs in wooded areas may be a factor in over-estimating coyote populations. Not only are the tracks of dogs similar to those of coyotes but dogs are well-known deer killers."

However, I had hunted bobcats in the area since the 1930s and until the winter of 1962, the only dog-like tracks I ever saw there were those made by my hounds or the hounds of the few other parties I encountered.

The first successful coyote trapping by John Wagg and Bill Lane in the area confirmed my belief that a new predator was present, leading me to conclude that the decline of deer that began in the late 1960s was related to the increase in coyotes.

Although deer kills that could positively be attributed to coyotes continued in succeeding winters, the Fisheries-Wildlife Department rejected a proposal to subsidize Wagg and Lane in trapping coyotes. Whether it would have prevented or delayed the spread of coyotes is conjecture, but there is evidence that John Guptill, a veteran trapper, and the late Warden Basil Closson, succeeded in stemming an invasion of smaller coyotes

Bud Wagg and Bob Lane walking back to their woods buggy with first two coyotes trapped in the Spencer Lake (Jackman region.) The animals were small compared with others caught later and weighed about 23 pounds.

in the Frankfort area, back in the late 1940s. (see Chapter Eight)

The "meat" of the study by the Colby students follows:

"There seems to be good evidence that coyotes travel in pairs during the winter months. All of the coyotes tracked for any distance were in groups of two. Occasionally individual tracks were observed but these were only those tracks followed for a very short distance. Another exception reported by Warden

Bud Wagg and Bob Lane in their woods buggy they were using to trap beaver in the Spencer Lake area near Jackman. Asked to try for the strange animal that had appeared in the region, they caught two the first night they set. Had they been subsidized, they would have continued to trap for coyotes and perhaps delayed their spread.

Carroll Goodwin on January 26 involved three sets of tracks together in the area of Fish Pond. Most often, however, paired tracks remained together for a time, then split for a short distance and rejoined. The above seems especially reasonable since mating occurs in January and February.

"During the month of January, two deer kills were investigated and used as a starting point for tracking . . . On January 21 a dead fawn was discovered on the northwest flank of Cathcart Mountain. A number of coyote tracks were noted in the area. The deer's ribs and a portion of the intestines had been exposed and one foreleg had been carried away. As it was late, the kill was marked and returned to on January 22. On that date the dead deer and surrounding area were further studied.

"The deer measured 40 inches from nose to rump and lay in a depression containing deer droppings. The deer appeared to be very thin and not extremely healthy. (A Mr. Quirion, snowmobiling in the area, noted that he was a deer hunter and after observing the dead deer stated that it didn't appear very healthy.)

"The deer's intestines had been pulled out more than on January 21, but it did not appear that coyotes had returned to the kill, although fresh tracks were discovered some distance away. Canada jays were observed scavenging at the kill and carrying away small pieces of intestine. Two sets of coyote tracks were backtracked from the area and observed to have entered at a walking pace. One approached an apparent deer bedding area about 80 feet upslope from the kill. The coyote tracks appeared to break into a running gait just adjacent to this area and seemed to follow a set of running deer tracks into the kill area. Large holes were observed just behind the kill where the deer may have stumbled. From the walking gait of the coyotes until almost at the bedding area and the fact that none of the other deer tracks in the area indicated running, it seems likely that the coyotes surprised the fawn while resting and chased it but a short distance. A slightly bloody area was found a short distance away where it appeared a coyote had paused to eat.

"Another deer kill was discovered by Carroll Goodwin on January 22 northeast of Whipple Farm in the Long Pond area. On January 24, Goodwin led us to the area which was an area of cedars and other softwoods. The kill was a buck of average size and lay in a large muddy pit with water at the bottom. Goodwin postulated that the deer had been killed on the night of January 21 when it broke through into the large spring hole while being pursued by coyotes. Only the rump and tail of the deer had been eaten away. A number of coyote prints were found around the kill, some of which Goodwin felt were left since he had last visited the kill. A set of tracks was followed onto a small hill above the area and then back past the kill. Tracks leaving the kill area indicated a very fast gallop with leaps of eight to nine feet measured.

"It seems likely that the coyotes were scared away from the kill at some time, since the coyotes continued to run for a considerable distance. On January 25, only fox tracks were discovered near the kill, some of which may have eaten off the deer. On January 26, coyote tracks were discovered circling around the kill area and leaving, but not approaching the kill itself. On January 27, a lower foreleg was taken from this deer for analysis of bone marrow.

"From studying the above two kills, it seems likely that coyotes are very wary of man. In both cases, it appears that the kills were abandoned after man had entered the area. In addition, tracks were observed to later come near both kills but not to the kill itself. It is possible that after a longer time the coyotes would return to the kills, as they have usually been known to completely devour kills.

"Examples of feeding by coyotes on species other than deer were found in only one case. On January 27, a sample of a scat (droppings) was found while following coyote tracks. The sample appeared to contain bones of a bird or small mammal.

Teeth of northeastern coyote are examined by trappers Bud Wagg and Walter Lane. John Guptill of Frankfort, a veteran trapper, first noticed that the principal fangs turned inside at the tip, different than those of domestic dogs which are straighter.

Goodwin, however, did report finding squirrel, muskrat and rabbit kills by coyotes in the Fish Pond area on January 26. The fact that remains of small mammals, usually part of the coyote's diet, were not discovered may be due to their smaller size in contrast to deer which are difficult to miss. In addition, observations were prejudiced by the fact that a considerable amount of tracking was begun at deer kills and then covered only the small distance from these kills possible to cover on foot. Hopefully analysis of scats will provide more precise evidence of diet, although only a very small number of scats was collected.

"The small number of observations which we were able to make during this study provides little basis for many definitive conclusions. It does seem fairly certain that coyotes tend to hunt and travel in pairs during the winter. Time, tracking conditions, and limitations of winter travel made it difficult to determine winter range, however, 8-10 miles would probably be a conservative estimate. There is also good evidence that coyotes are wary of man and easily scared from deer kills.

"The winter diet of the Maine coyote almost certainly includes deer but little else is certain. Hopefully, analysis of scats will provide some information. Regarding feeding by coyotes on deer, further study should be done to determine several important aspects. The most important of these is the condition of deer killed and/or eaten. In Adolph Murie's thorough study, *Ecology of the Coyote in the Yellowstone*, a number of factors regarding coyote-deer relationships were discovered.

"Among the important points made by Murie was the well-known fact that winter is extremely hard on deer, many of which do not survive. Others become very sick and weak, with their survival merely lessening the overall health of the deer herd. Coyotes may perform an important function in an ecosystem by eliminating the sick and weak and disposing of carrion which may be a possible source of disease. Unless the former state of health of a dead deer is determined, coyote tracks around a carcass mean little, and certainly not that coyotes are destroying deer herds.

"In conclusion, we feel that this study has fulfilled at least one of the two purposes mentioned in the introduction. It has proved to be a valuable learning experience for its participants. A great deal has been learned about tracking and wildlife. As far as the second purpose is concerned, we hope that some useful information has been added to what is known about the Maine coyote."

I would have to partly agree with the conclusions of the study report. Even under ideal conditions, one month's observations by three persons not thoroughly experienced in tracking would hardly form the basis of a definite report on the relationship between the coyote and deer in Maine.

Voit Richens was among the first scientific researchers of the northeastern coyote when it made its appearance in Maine. In picture above he is examining skulls of canids to determine their identity. (University of Maine photo.)

Before heavy trapping removed more than 1,500 coyotes from areas where I hunt bobcat, I often found evidence of three to five traveling together. On many occasions, I followed coyote tracks on wood hauling roads for distances of up to 15 miles. Some groups of two and three apparently traveled several miles from an area containing no deer to places where they eventually made deer kills.

My observations, supported by research, also indicate that coyotes often remain in an area of dense snowshoe hare populations for several days to feed on rabbits.

In the fall of 1979 new research projects on fur-bearing animals, including the coyote, were started in Maine. Unfortunately, the results aren't expected to reveal anything not already known to experienced outdoorsmen. Such studies are conducted by the Wildlife Cooperative Unit based at the University of Maine at Orono. The unit works in cooperation with the state's Fisheries and Wildlife Department, which can and does provide equipment, manpower and expertise.

The projects have been defended by Lee E. Perry, assistant chief of the Maine Game Division. He contends that "black and white" data are needed to wrestle with the federal bureaucracy. At several public hearings he has agreed there are knowledgeable, practical wildlife observers in Maine but said their accumulated experience is of little value to modern researchers, particularly those on federal payrolls.

Most of the field research is done by students — devoted, enthusiastic individuals in the process of gaining from experience what many practical hunters, trappers and observers have accumulated through years of activity.

How unfortunate for the cause of wildlife that the practical and technical factions cannot come to a mutual understanding and agree to cooperate. Both may have the same objective, but they are following paths that lead them further apart each year.

Lester McCann of the Biology Department, College of St. Paul, Minnesota, whose book, "A New Day for Wildlife," is most provocative because it stresses the need for predator control and for listening more to the practicalists, describes the breach between these factions as unfortunate and a barrier to sound wildlife management.

So while the scientific branch of the Fisheries-Wildlife Department monitors live coyotes, the department's practicalists will continue coyote control programs in areas where they are detrimental to deer. It's a conflict difficult to fathom.

Walter Trundy, left, of Northport shot these smaller edition of "coyotes," then identified as coydogs that had appeared in a Waldo County area in the 1940s. Warden Leon Gilpatrick checked the animals which were later autopsied at the University of Maine laboratory.

Some northeastern coyotes become trophies of the hunt. Here are four of them mounted by Simon Gagnon of Hinckley. They came from different parts of the state, mostly north of Skowhegan.

This is a typical logging road near Basin Pond, Somerset County, where the Wildlife Research unit began studying fur-bearers, including coyotes in 1979. Once holding upwards of 80 wintering deer, it was a novelty to spot a deer track during the 1980-81 winter.

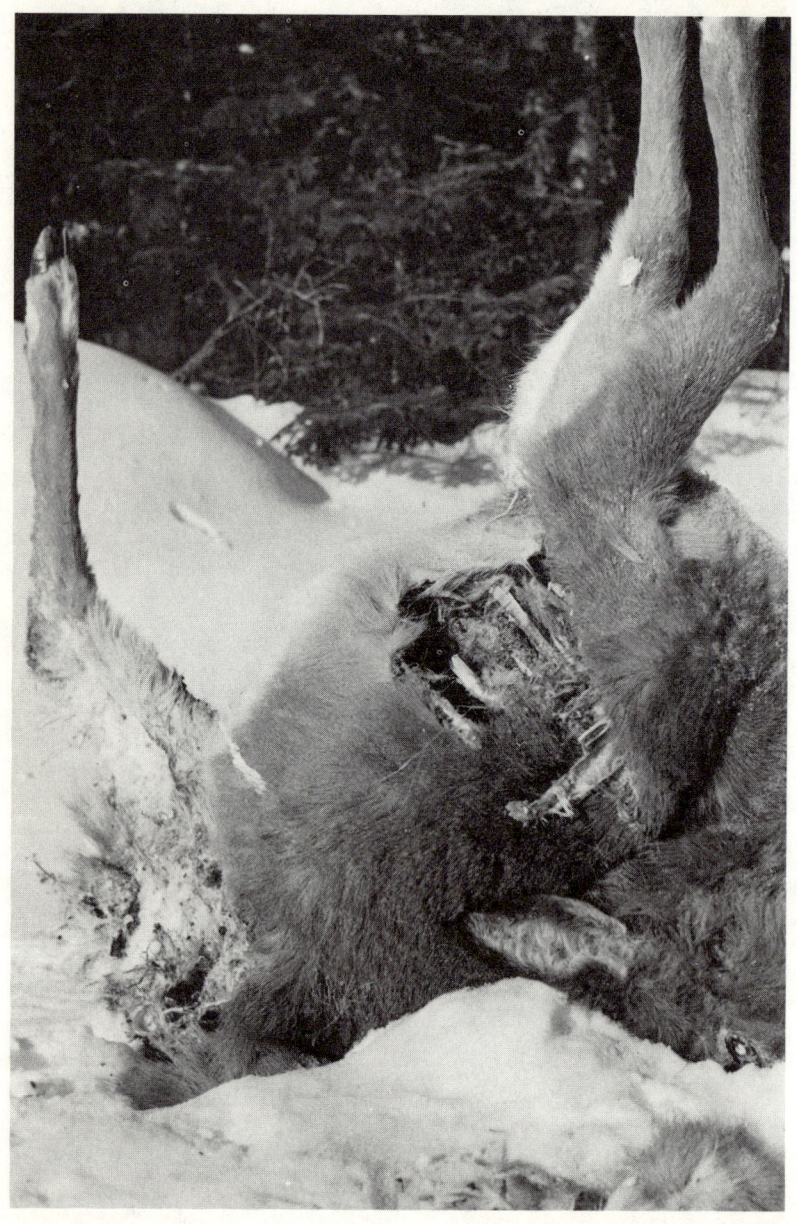

Good specimen of deer killed by coyotes was this yearling buck at Cambridge which Warden Norman Gilbert and the writer examined on January 22, 1977. Note partly eaten hindquarters and ribs.

Feeding Habits

Perhaps the only universally accepted fact concerning Maine's new predator is that it isn't fussy about its diet.

The northeastern coyote will feed on anything from cricket to mouse, grouse, rabbit, deer, moose, chickens, domestic cats and lambs, live fish and almost any variety of berries and fruits.

Biological experts classify the mixed-breed canid as an opportunist. Laymen with any amount of wildlife experience agree.

During the early part of the animal's invasion of Maine, the stomachs of 51 coyote carcasses were analyzed by Voit B. Richens of the Maine Cooperative Wildlife Research Unit, Orono, and Roy Hugie, a biologist. A report compiled in 1974 by Richens and Henry Hilton, then of the School of Forest Resources, and later named fur-bearing animal planner with the Fisheries-Wildlife Department, summarized what was found in the 51 animals taken in Maine as well as 113 from other New England states, nearly all of which were killed in the fall-early winter period.

The report concluded that coyotes did not depend on two or three major foods but "opportunistically took whatever was abundant and available." White-tailed deer remains found in the stomachs were generally considered to be carrion, which is relatively abundant following the deer hunting season.

The authors also surmised that "if availability largely determines food taken by these canids, then coyotes in remote areas should consume different foods or foods in different proportions than those in settled areas. Coyote-prey relationships and the impact of coyotes on prey populations has not yet been evaluated in New England."

Hilton and Richens conducted a subsequent study in the remote St. John-Allagash Wilderness of western Aroostook County during the winter of 1974-75. A summary of their findings noted that the diet of Maine coyotes "appears to vary with availability and abundance of food at different seasons and in

Although supposed to exude very little scent, fawn deer as the one above, normally drop wherever they happen to be if the doe gives them the warning signal, and become vulnerable to predation. This particular fawn dropped on an abandoned hauling road as a jeep approached and would have been easy target for any species of predator.

different regions. In settled areas, coyotes eat a great variety of items including refuse, fruit, unretrieved hunter-killed deer and domestic stock remains. In remote, unsettled areas, coyotes appear to scavenge less and become more predatory, depending more heavily on deer, hare, and other wild animals."

The study covered six townships along the Big Black and St.

John rivers. The area has an average total snowfall of 96 inches and a mean winter temperature of 18 degrees F. The objective was to evaluate coyote feeding habits and prey relationships throughout the year in an environment of minimal human disturbance. The report is based on eight weeks of "intensive snow tracking and examination of 138 winter and spring scats and 41 fall-early winter stomachs. A total of 32 coyote tracks were followed 95 miles during January and the first week of February, 1975.

The following abstract is taken from the report:

"Ninety percent of the coyote tracks followed went through areas of high hare density. A typical tactic for lone coyotes was to walk directly into a thicket and then pursue the flushed hare. Of coyotes which hunted in pairs, one animal appeared to walk through clearings such as roadways while its companion dashed into brush and other cover to drive the hare in its direction. The success rate seemed higher for paired coyotes than for singles. Of all tracks followed, only 16 percent led to at least one kill. Persistent hunting rather than high success rate may account for the high frequency, 34 percent, of hare in scats for all periods.

"Squirrels were encountered by coyotes in virtually all habitats and frequently were pursued. The capture success rate could not be measured but the low frequency of occurrence in scat suggested that squirrels were an elusive prey for coyotes.

"Only nine percent of the coyote tracks suggested small mammal hunting by these canids. Such activity was indicated by diggings in snowbanks, into brush piles and around tree stumps. The importance of small mammals to coyotes in Maine is unknown. However, the data appear to support the conclusion by D. D. Green in 1951 (Modern Methods of Predator Control) that coyotes have little effect on population cycles of rodents and lagomorphs, the latter including gnawing animals such as hares.

"Coyotes, both singly and in pairs, showed considerable interest in beaver and otter holes in the river and stream ice where muskrats could emerge. Coyote beds were often located in spots from which these holes could be readily observed. (Blaine Lambert, a veteran Aroostook County trapper, reported that during the winter of 1980-81, he found where at least eight beavers in a colony had been attacked and killed by coyotes.)

"The frequency of muskrat remains in scats (17 percent) and the low number of muskrat tracks observed suggest high vulnerability of exposed muskrats to coyote predation. Muskrats would be especially vulnerable during dispersal movements; twice as many muskrat remains occurred in summer-early fall scats as in scats deposited at other times.

"Occasionally remains of beaver, skunk and porcupine also appeared in coyote scats. Snow tracking suggested that little time was spent by coyotes actively hunting for these animals. Ruffed grouse are abundant in the study area but only one instance of predation was observed. The relatively rare occurrence of grouse and other bird remains in scats supports the conclusion that these animals are infrequent food items."

The study further notes that "coyotes intersect deer tracks frequently and they presumably see deer often." It notes, too, that coyotes traveling in pairs or packs "accounted for only 11 percent of recorded intersections but 85 percent of the pursuits.

"Interpretation of signs at one deer kill suggested that several coyotes met a single male deer and made physical contact within 25 yards after beginning the pursuit. The pursuit continued for 500 yards with frequent attacks indicated by the presence of deer skin and hair along the route. The deer was killed at the bottom of a steep bank at the edge of the Big Black River; it was 9.5 years old (determined by tooth sectioning) and had a bone marrow fat content of about 75 percent based on marrow color and consistency. (A pink marrow usually occurs in a healthy deer while a reddish marrow indicates nutrition deficiency.)

"An observation by Warden Rodney Sirois on the St. John River during the summer showed that single deer can successfully elude an attack by a single coyote. The coyote chased a doe out of shallow water onto the riverbank but she suddenly turned and ran back into three feet of water and faced the attacking coyote.

"At this water depth the coyote was forced to swim and it discontinued the attack, swam to shore and after watching for several minutes walked into the woods. The doe remained vigilant in the water for more than 30 minutes before it ran into the woods on the opposite shore."

Seven deer kills were located in the area studied by Hilton and Richens. They reported all apparently involved more than one coyote pursuing a single deer and terminated in cut-over areas or on the ice.

Their report noted: "Snowshoe hare remains were found in 34 percent of winter and summer scats from the study area, and hare is probably the principal prey species for coyotes in the area.

"The abundance of red squirrels throughout the state is not known but the low frequency of remains in scats from the study area suggests that they are unimportant in the diet of coyotes.

"Beaver remains found in scats may represent carrion resulting from trapped beaver carcasses discarded in winter and from mortality resulting from ice floes in the spring on the major rivers... Otherwise their infrequent occurrence in scats probably represented rare chance associations where circumstances permitted a kill.

"Song birds and grouse remains were infrequent in scats and there was little evidence to suggest their being hunted extensively by coyotes.

"A high frequency of deer remains in scats, 42 percent, and a marked seasonal difference, 24 percent in summer and 53 percent in winter, suggests that availability of carrion in winter, vulnerability of fawns in spring and the greater mobility of deer in summer contribute to the variation in deer consumption by coyotes. However, much additional data are needed to clarify this.

"A relatively low statewide abundance of hare and the small number of coyote stomachs examined probably accounts for the lack of snowshoe hare remains found in the stomachs during the fall-early winter period. Conversely, their abundance on the study area from which most scats were collected probably is a factor in their higher frequency noted in scats.

"Small mammals appear to be taken according to abundance and availability. Contents of stomach samples suggest that in the fall and in agricultural areas, small mammals are most important in the coyote diet than in the winter in forested areas.

"Deer remains in the stomachs sampled suggest that in settled areas where deer carrion is available it is eaten while in wild areas with few hunter-killed deer, coyotes rely more heavily on killing natural live prey, i.e., they scavenge less and increase their predatory tendencies.

"The differential feeding habit is related to the availability and abundance of particular food items, characteristic of an opportunistic carnivore. It is not inferred or suggested that coyotes control or suppress wild animal populations in remote areas. However, these data emphasize that there is a complex and intricate coyote-prey relationship which should be recognized and thoroughly investigated."

Following are tables of food habits compiled by Maine researchers:

Table 1. Food habits of Maine coyotes as determined by examination of 138 winter-spring scats and 82 summer scats, 1974-75.

Food Item	Number of Occurrences In Scats W-S	S	% Occurrence W-S	S
White-tailed deer (*Odocoileus virginianus*)	74	20	53.6	24.4
Snowshoe hare (*Lepus americana*)	48	28	34.8	34.1
Red squirrel (*Tamiasciurus hudsonicus*)	17	2	12.3	2.4
Small mammals (*Rodentia, Insectivora*)	8	10	5.7	12.2
Muskrat (*Ondatra zibethica*)	7	10	5.1	12.2
Other mammals (*Erethizon, Marmota, Alces Mephitis, Castor*)	8	11	5.7	13.4
Birds (*Calliformes, Passeriformes*)	0	4	0.0	4.9
Plant material (*Picea, Graminae, Poaceae, Malus, Prunus*)	35	11	25.4	13.4
Unidentified	3	3	2.2	3.7

W-S = winter-spring
S = summer

Table 2. Food habits of Maine coyotes as determined from examination of 30 stomachs, 1974-75.

Food Item	Number of Occurrences In Stomachs	% Occurrence
White-tailed deer *(Odocoileus virginianus)*	10	33.3
Small mammals *(Clethrionomys, Napeozapus, Peromyseus)*	8	26.6
Fruit *(Malus, Vaccinium)*	5	16.7
Plant material *(Graminae)*	7	23.3
Miscellaneous & unidentified*	9	30.0

*This includes trap debris, a canid toe, garbage, known carrion and Diptera larvae.

Food habits of coyotes in Maine always have been a subject of confusion and argument. Many of the stomachs taken for analysis have been from coyotes killed in seasons other than winter. Parts of a letter dated Dec. 5, 1972 and written by Voit B. Richens, assistant leader of the Maine Cooperative Wildlife Research Unit, to J. William Peppard, deputy commissioner of the Fisheries-Wildlife Department, indicate that deer play a complex role in the diet of coyotes. It draws on a study of 24 stomachs:

". . . deer composed nearly 100 percent of some stomach contents and very little in others. Fly maggots were found in some stomachs containing deer meat, evidence that the coyotes ate some deer carrion.

"We don't know why rodents form such a small part of the coyote diet but presumably this is due to availability of deer carrion and hare. Most coyotes have been collected during or following the deer hunting season when unretrieved hunter kills are available in the woods. One coyote stomach contained nothing but domestic 'cow,' all carrion. Fifty-nine percent of one stomach content was black bear and 99 percent of another red fox; the bear was certainly carrion and probably also the fox.

"Most of the insect material was grasshoppers and crickets. The fruit was mostly apples and the avian material was all songbird. The high frequency of occurrence for vegetation is undoubtedly related to accidental ingestion with other foods, although in some cases the coyote apparently chose to eat it.

". . . Seven stomachs were entirely empty, 3 had very little food in them, and 3 carcasses had the stomachs removed before we received them. More coyotes are now being trapped and seldom do trapped animals have much in their stomachs when they are killed.

Foods from 24 Maine Coyote Stomachs, 1968-1972

Food Item	% of Total Wt. (Air Dry)	% Occurrence
Deer	24.7	37.5
Hare	21.9	25.0
Rodents	0.9	12.5
Cattle	8.5	4.6
Birds	tr.	25.0
Insects	3.1	20.8
Fruit	1.5	20.8
Plants	2.2	58.3
*Other	34.0	58.0
Total	100.0	— —

*Includes bear, coyote, porcupine quills, red fox, moose, raccoon, maggots, paper, tin foil, bone, a trap pan cover and unidentifiable material.

A new and broader study of coyotes began in Maine in the fall of 1979 in Hancock and Washington counties as part of an overall predator-ecology project. Another study, designed to determine predation and its effect on game species and livestock was launched in the Pierce Pond area of Somerset County.

Two articles in the winter, 1981, issue of the Fisheries-Wildlife Department's magazine reported on the progress of these programs.

Suzanne L. Caturano and Daniel J. Harrison, graduate assistants at the Maine Cooperative Wildlife Research Unit, Orono, reporting on the Hancock-Washington area study, noted that a "detailed examination of 573 scats (droppings) we collected, showed coyotes fed on snowshoe hare consistently, the year round. Although evidence of deer and hare appears in scats collected during the winter and spring, the occurrence of deer drops off to a very low level during summer and fall and is substituted by fruit, mainly blueberries, and small mammals."

While neither article reports any deer kills by coyotes, particularly in the Pierce Pond area where several have been discovered in past years, it seems natural to wonder whether the decline of deer has simply made them less available.

The leader of the Maine Wildlife Research Unit, James A. Sherburne, notes in closing that when analyses of data are completed "we should be able to make a valuable contribution of basic data needed in making decisions on several important species of wildlife. We can also expect the results of this study to present new and interesting challenges and to identify some remaining key questions to be answered in the quest for a more complete and thorough understanding of this fascinating furbearer community."

Food habits of the coyotes thus have been under scrutiny for many years — since 1968 in Maine — and the results have been relatively clear-cut and consistent. Whether such research should continue indefinitely is among the questions the "evaluation committee" appointed by Commissioner Manuel will have to decide.

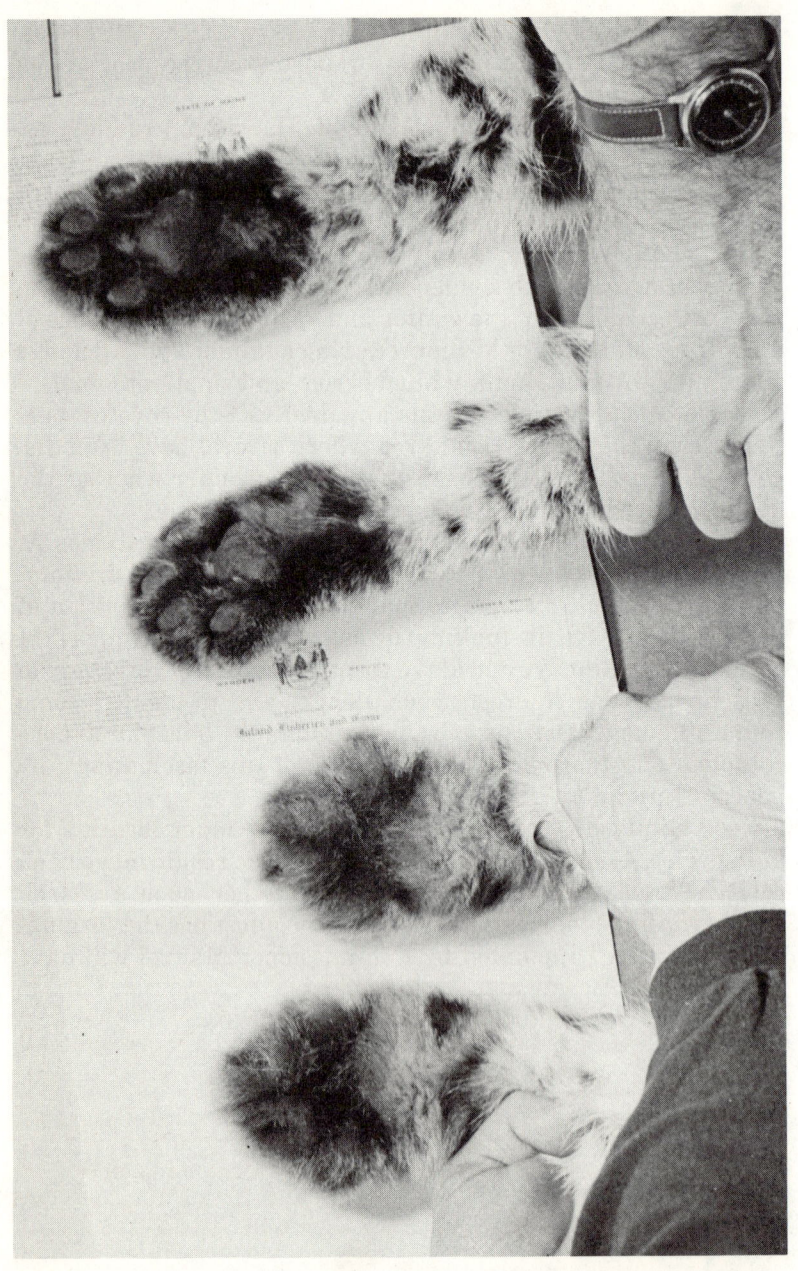

Difference in feet of Canada lynx and bobcat is revealed in this photo by Maine Fisheries-Wildlife Department. At left, lynx shows no pads as feet are covered entirely by fur. Right, bobcat's pads and heel can be seen exposed. Under certain snow conditions track of lynx can be mistaken for that of coyote.

How Predators Kill

Methods of stalking and killing white-tailed deer by predators and domestic animals in Maine vary, but there are definite ways of pinpointing responsibility for most kills.

If I were to note every dead deer I have come upon in the Maine woods during the past 50 years, this book would take on the proportions of a dictionary. Consequently, I will limit the discussion to a few specific examples that best reveal what years of observation have taught me about deer kills by bobcats, coyotes, domestic dogs and bears.

Having hunted bobcats for 30 years before coming upon a coyote track in Maine, I can confidently say you are more likely to find deer kills by following a hound on bobcat tracks, than by picking one or more coyote tracks and following them without help from a dog.

The serious bobcat hunter expects at times to discover that his prey has killed a deer. Conversely, most deer kills by coyotes are found accidentally while following bobcat hounds or reported by others frequently in the woods.

The stalking of a deer by bobcat usually is not prolonged and may best be described as ambushing. Once in an area populated by deer, a bobcat may stalk from bed to bed or find a hiding place next to a deer run and wait for one to show. The bobcat probably is more effective when there is snow on the ground, although little is known about its deer-stalking habits in other seasons.

A fairly typical example of a single bobcat ambush of deer occurred in the Dead River region, within a mile of quarters occupied at the time by Arthur Haskell, who has since retired after being gate controller at Flagstaff Dam for many years.

I was hunting alone with one of my hounds when I noticed a bobcat track crossing the Long Falls Dam road and heading in the direction of a comparatively small patch of woods behind the caretaker's home. On a number of occasions I had chatted with Haskell and his wife and had reason to believe Mrs. Haskell wasn't convinced that even a small, 20-pound bobcat could kill an adult deer.

As always, I checked the track thoroughly to make sure the animal had not backtracked within its own trail — something that happens occasionally — and followed it into the woods for perhaps a hundred yards before discovering a fresh deer kill. The fact that the bobcat had fed on the animal and covered it with hair indicated the kill had been made a few hours before I came upon it. I alerted the Haskells, who both showed keen interest in my find and accompanied me to the spot to see some first-hand proof of the bobcat's prowess.

I retraced the track of the dead deer, which was mixed with at least three other whitetails, and found the beaten snow path where the bobcat had waited for its prey, hiding itself behind a thick growth of low softwoods. The evidence indicated that the bobcat had allowed all the deer to walk by before emerging from its cover and bounding upon the back of the last deer. The actual distance of the chase was only 20 feet, two bounds. The deer, an adult doe, fell within 50 feet of the attack. Skinning the deer's neck, I discovered that the bobcat had bitten into the main artery, opening holes on both sides of the neck. It had eaten part of a ham and loin then covered the kill with deer hair and small bushes.

Ordinarily a kill of this type means the bobcat will be returning for one or more feeds — if it is not disturbed or driven away by fishers or coyotes.

Under favorable trailing conditions, any of my dogs would readily overtake such a bobcat. But on this day the snow was melting fast into the crust, the temperature was rising and water was seeping into the tracks, washing away the scent. Lead, the hound I was hunting that day, found hard going when the trail led to ice bordering the nearby Dead River. The dog eventually lost distance and I had to call him off.

I also found evidence of a bobcat stalking deer while perched on a tree limb overhanging a deer trail in fairly deep snow. This is a case of hit or miss on the part of the bobcat, and on some occasions I have seen where, even after scoring a hit, the bobcat was thwarted when the deer rolled several times on the ground, shaking its assailant and running to safety.

Not so typical incidents included finding four deer killed the same night — according to the evidence on the fresh snow — by a single, 35-pound male bobcat. It occurred in the town of Starks where later I found a family of four other bobcats feeding on the kills. Apparently the male was hunting for the others in the family.

I also found in the Burrill Woods of Canaan an instance in which two bobcats overtook two deer, after tracking them for two miles, killing both almost side by side. They took one meal and as far as I could discover never returned.

Bobcats do not always feed on rump or loins. Some will open the chest cavity and pull out the lungs and heart, which they seem to prefer for an opening meal.

After examining hundreds of deer kills, I feel certain that bobcats take deer as they come rather than stalking only the

Not all deer succumb to dog or predator attack. This doe, from which several dogs were driven, made it through the winter with the help of retired Warden Harold Turkey of Belgrade. (Photo by Arthur G. Rogers.)

old, sick and weak. A similar conclusion was reached by biologist Merwin Marston of the Maine Fisheries-Wildlife Department, who studied 46 deer killed by bobcats during the winter of 1943-44. In fact, I have never come upon what I would consider an unhealthy deer that had been killed either by a bobcat or, in recent years, by a coyote.

From 1945 to the early 1960s when deer were plentiful in areas I hunted, it wasn't uncommon for bobcats to spend long periods where deer were yarded in the winter. As deer declined, the bobcats traveled farther. They increased their range even more when the price of their pelts skyrocketed and hunting pressure doubled.

There are instances when signs show that bobcats sometimes fail to kill deer, even after terrific battles. But the ability of an average size bobcat to jump a deer and pierce its jugular vein cannot be disputed. If there is such a thing as "humane" killing in predation, the bobcat is most merciful where deer are concerned; coyotes are the most merciless, domestic dogs the most senseless.

Deer, when attacked, are most likely to act like sheep, giving way to fear. There are exceptions, of course, and frequently a deer will throw a bobcat from its back by rolling over and manage to get away. But once the bobcat bites into the jugular, death follows quickly.

Coyotes and dogs run after deer until they overtake them or until the deer find an avenue of escape, such as open water, a rare occurrence during Maine winters.

Coyotes will start feeding on a downed deer before it has expired. Dogs, having bitten into the rump of deer they were chasing, often attack the deer's neck and throat to kill it. It is not unusual for dogs not to feed on deer they have run down, which differ from coyote habits. But a pack of dogs can race through a deer yard and destroy several animals before returning home to be petted.

I was in the Spencer Lake region west of Jackman the first time I stumbled onto a deer that had been killed by coyotes. I was amazed to find the ribs had been eaten down to the backbone. It clearly was not the work of bobcats or dogs. I had examined enough deer kills by both to be sure they could not crack ribs. On a few occasions, in late March, I had come upon deer carcasses with missing ribs which I presumed bears had eaten.

Although an ongoing research project by the University of Maine Wildlife Unit had failed, when this was written, to find evidence of a multiple deer kill by coyotes, I began noting them that same winter. Since then I have been able to confirm kills of four to twelve deer in the Allagash region, Dallas Plantation, North Dexter, Ashland, Canaan, Ten Thousand Acre Tract, Indian Pond (The Forks), Pierce Pond Township, Unity and Starks.

During the winter of 1977, Earl Shaw of Unity, an experienced bobcat hunter, found 17 dead deer in Unity Plantation. Believing they had been killed by coyotes, he contacted the

Fisheries-Wildlife Department and guided a representative to the site to check the carcasses. The kill never was officially confirmed. Nor was responsibility ever attributed to causes other than that determined by Shaw.

Coyotes most often record deer kills after chases of less than several hundred feet. But they also have plenty of patience. I have tracked them following deer several miles without making a kill. An example of that persistence occurred in the Flagstaff Lake area and, coincidentally, also involved Arthur Haskell.

While hunting bobcats north of Highland Plantation, I came upon the tracks of three coyotes crossing the road at the south end of Flagstaff Lake. They were following a single deer, a fairly large animal according to the tracks, which was heading north toward Flagstaff Dam. Since coyote tracks were becoming more common, I gave the matter no further thought and continued searching for a fresh bobcat track.

Two days later I visited the same area and learned that Haskell and his wife had seen an antlered deer being chased by three coyotes on the lake. Although the chase was too distant for Haskell to shoot and kill any of the coyotes, he emptied a clip from his rifle, hoping it would make them stop. The ruse worked. The coyotes darted for the nearby woods while the deer continued west in the direction of the Spring Lake road.

While checking that road the following day I drove across Long Falls Dam on Dead River toward Spring Lake. Less than a mile from the dam I noticed a bloody mess in the snow. Spotting the tracks of a single deer and several coyotes, I decided to investigate further. Following the tracks for a short distance I came upon a large, male deer, still alive despite the fact its hindquarters were nearly missing. I did not have to guess what had happened. The three coyotes the Haskells had seen chasing the deer had resumed their stalk and overtaken their prey. Two woodsmen who came upon this scene humanely killed the deer.

That same winter I came upon two woodsmen dressing a freshly killed doe in the same area. They had driven two coyotes from the carcass and planned to salvage the venison for their own use.

On February 26, 1980 I met biologist John Dryska in the Pierce Pond region in the same general area. He was trying to make radio contact with coyotes and bobcats during the second stage of a research project on fur-bearing animals in the area. There were about three inches of snow on the ground, and when

Biologist Gene Dumont, foreground, and Bertram Nelson, look over one of 11 deer killed in Sibley Bog, near Canaan, by coyotes. I made this picture on March 1, 1977 and noted that six of the does killed were carrying twin fawns.

I came upon tracks of two coyotes following a single deer, I decided to investigate.

The tracks, heading east, crossed the Appalachian Trail north of the East Carry Pond road in the direction of Wyman Lake where much of the snow had been blown from the surface,

Spread-eagling on slippery ice, such as shown above, as this doe deer did at East Pond in the Belgrade Lakes region, usually proves deadly. But if uninjured, as this deer, it can be towed to shoreline, regain its feet and go on its way. That's how Arthur G. Rogers, retired warden supervisor, found this doe and saved her.

leaving a slippery, glare ice. On that surface, the coyotes had easily overtaken and killed the deer, eaten both hams and part of the loins.

A few days later, I was informed by Chester McKay of West Forks that three other dead deer had been found on the lake, not far from the fresh kill. Before the winter was over, two more deer were reported killed on Wyman Lake by coyotes.

Glare ice is a death trap for deer. Once on it, their ability to walk or run is greatly impaired. They usually "split" or "spread-eagle" and once down simply cannot get back on their feet.

In all of these coyote stalks on deer, the predators attacked first from the rear, often ripping off chunks of flesh that they stopped to eat before continuing the chase. But the evidence that most often points to coyotes as culprits in a deer kill is their ability to break and eat the ribs. I have checked kills with woodsmen and game wardens for 20 years, and the remains are always similar.

Deer that escape pursuit by coyotes usually do so by finding open water. One area where this happens in winter is at the confluence of the Dead and Kennebec rivers. Several persons have witnessed deer braving the icy water to foil one or more pursuing coyotes.

Domestic dogs nearly duplicate the pattern of coyotes when running down deer although there can be differences depending on the makeup of the pack.

During a winter several years ago an "epidemic" of deer kills by dogs occurred in the South China area where the late Olin Jackson was game warden. Using air and ground crews, a special team from the Maine Fisheries-Wildlife Department was able to eliminate the dog pack, which consisted of four rather small dogs of different breeds. The pack was led by a cross-bred hound, which apparently had tracking ability. The other dogs were silent trailers, much the same as most coyotes, and according to the wardens, did the killing.

One difference between dog packs and coyotes I have noticed is that dogs seldom feed on deer for any length of time following a kill. They generally prefer to search for another deer to chase. Coyotes often feed on a deer as long as there is meat left, leaving only when disturbed by humans.

Coyotes will howl on some chases but their yipping at night often isn't associated with a hunt.

One of the differences between the final attack on a deer by dogs and coyotes is that dogs often will bring a deer down by biting its ears and head. I have never noted severe head or ear injuries when examining deer killed by coyotes.

Another mongrel pack was found at Brown's Corner in Canaan during the winter of 1977. While laboratory examinations leaned toward a finding that four were dogs, one had brain and skull features similar to that of a coyote. The pack was killing deer by chasing them and attacking from the rear. They also frequently returned to feed on their prey, making me think they were mixed coyote-dog. As has been noted elsewhere, coyote-dog crosses most often resemble dogs.

Domestic dogs contribute to the deer predation in Maine. In photo above Warden Charles Davis holds one of several fawns removed from six deer killed by two pet dogs at Indian Pond/The Forks, during the winter of 1978-79. The dogs had roamed away from Squaw Mountain ski area into one of the better deer yards in the Greenville region.

My knowledge of bear in relation to deer predation is minimal. I can recall only one instance where a bear actually picked up a fawn and began carrying it off. It occurred in Township Nine, Range 14 where the late Jim Clarkson was caretaker. One of the Allagash region's most colorful characters, Clarkson became better known when he assumed care of Lock Dam between Chamberlain and Eagle lakes.

I was visiting Jim, having walked to his camp on Russell Brook from the Tramway at Eagle Lake, nine miles to the south. When he heard the fawn and doe bleat, he grabbed his .45 caliber revolver, ran toward the bear and shot it dead. The fawn returned to its mother.

If bears kill many deer, the evidence has yet to be found. They do feed on carcasses they find in the spring, but during my fifty years in Maine's outdoors, I have yet to note the actual killing of a deer by a bear.

It would be a simple matter for an adult bear to kill a deer — were he able to catch the more fleet-footed animal — either by striking it with a paw or crushing it with its front legs.

Bears den in Maine from early fall through mid-March, sometimes later depending upon snow conditions and temperatures. They seldom leave their dens during the winter unless flooded out or disturbed. So they are no threat to whitetails during their winter yarding period.

I did find a bear one winter feeding on a deer. It was near Basin Pond, in Somerset County, where I was hunting bobcat. It was Jan. 4, 1968 and the snow was more than two feet deep. I had discovered a bobcat track in a deer trail and released two of my hounds, Belle and Jack, on it. They soon were out of hearing and I decided to use my snowmobile to catch up with them. I drove it over a large, snow-covered hardwood blowdown, overtook the chase and eventually killed the bobcat.

A week passed before I returned to the area. When I did, a group of Quebec woodsmen informed me that I had driven my snowmobile directly over an injured bear. I thought they were kidding, but they led me to the blowdown and showed me the remains of a deer. The injured bear had been leaving its den to feed on the deer, probably because of its weakened condition.

The woodsmen managed to capture the bear by fashioning a snare from telephone wire. As soon as the bear discovered they meant to help, it gave up without protest. They fed the bear warm milk, kept him in camp two days, then brought it to a veterinarian in St. George for treatment of a bullet wound in the hip, apparently inflicted during the fall hunting season. Later that winter I learned the bear had not recovered as the woodsmen had hoped.

I was unable to determine how the deer died, but it was obvious that the wounded bear could not have been responsible.

The state's leash law and a rigid vigil on roaming domestic dogs have contributed to a big decline in deer losses from household pets. However, little has been done to control coyotes, although there is no doubt that coyotes today are both the most common deer predators in Maine and, if degrees of humaneness are considered, the most cruel.

I found this 125-pound male deer on March 26, 1969 while hunting bobcats in the Bingham area. It was a perfect example of a kill by a bobcat. The fang mark which severed the jugular vein can be readily seen in the upper neck of the deer. Jim Jacques was with me when I took the picture. My hound Belle treed the responsible bobcat which weighed 26 pounds.

Perhaps the most distressing example of what happens when domestic dogs attack a deer was this doe which in Warden Leon Gilpatrick's words was "skinned alive." She was still breathing when he found her with half of her hide ripped off. (Photo by Arthur C. Rogers.)

Three mongrel dogs accounted for these deer in the South China area in January of 1970. With the guidance of pilot wardens a ground crew was able to round up the responsible dogs, but ten deer had been lost by that time. Warden Robert Rondeau, now in Springvale, and the late Olin Jackson, a warden at the time, are shown with the result of the roundup. Dog on top of deer, a mongrel, led the pack.

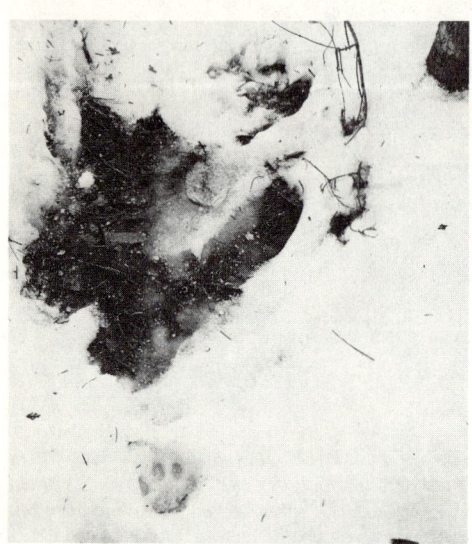

Snow texture and light conditions at the scene of a deer kill preclude photographing tracks so that they can be clearly defined. This picture, however, provided the ideal setting to photograph the track of the bobcat that had made the kill. The defined track can be seen at bottom of picture, the distinct four pads and the heel showing perfectly. Scene was in Deadwater area.

This is a perfect example of how a bobcat covers a deer kill if it intends to return to feed again on it. Hair stripped from deer is strewn completely over carcass thereby delaying the freezing of the meat. I took this picture while following my bobcat hounds — they led me to the kill — in upper Somerset County.

Brad Crafts of North Jay found the above remains of a large male deer killed in Redington Township, Franklin County, while he was snowmobiling in March. An experienced woodsman, Crafts said evidence in the snow indicated one coyote had jumped the deer out of a winter yard, chased it on a wood road where another coyote jumped from a bank and participated in the kill. Crafts noted that the theory that coyotes kill only the small and weak is "far fetched," that this deer was a big, healthy buck.

Although scarred on the left flank, this doe deer raised her fawn successfully in the Chase Stream area of Somerset County in 1968. After that, deer sightings dwindled steadily in that region as coyotes moved in from the west side of Route 201.

What About Winter Deer Kills?

During the 50 years I have attended seminars and public hearings on white-tailed deer in Maine, winter losses to the elements invariably became the prime subject and purported reason for major declines in deer populations. Members of the Game Division traditionally advance the winter loss theory even though their data fail to support it.

Deer die in the same manner as other animals, in all seasons of the year. In 60 years of walking, snowshoeing and snowmobiling over every county of the state, I have never seen evidence of a large deer kill that could be attributed to the winter elements. That isn't to say it hasn't happened.

Following the winter of 1933-34, the late Jim Clarkson, who lived alone in Township Nine, Range 14, deep in the Allagash region, led me to a deer "grave" where he estimated ten deer had died during a ten-day period of sub-zero temperatures, deep snow and high winds in late January. He felt the cold and snow combination had killed them although twice as many in the yard had survived.

And Skeet Davenport of Rangeley, a reliable, experienced outdoorsman and trapper, in the winter of 1968-69 found evidence of a large winter deer kill in the Kennebago region he knows so well. I have no reason to doubt the veracity of Davenport, but no scientific data were obtained from the kill even though it was reported to the proper authorities.

A memorandum to all game division personnel from Fred Gilbert, then in charge of deer management, on the subject of "Management Unit Quotas, 1971 deer season and other items," does little to advance the winter kill theory. At the time, the state was divided into eight "Ecological Zones" that since have changed in character and identification and now are referred to as wildlife units.

The memorandum "indicated" increased winter mortality in 1971 in Zone 1; normal winter mortality in Zone 2; severe winter mortality in Zone 3; increased winter mortality indicated in Zone 4; no unusual winter losses in Zone 5; indication of severe winter mortality in Zones 6 and 7; spring losses to dogs in Zone 7, and an indication of excessive late winter losses in Zone 8. Winter kill wasn't even among the categories on the table listing the major causes of deer mortality — other than legal kill — for the period from January of 1968 to June of 1971.

Following is a copy of that table:

Year	A	Cars	Dog	Illegal	Crop Protection	Miscellaneous	Total
1968		390	83	10	1	110	594
1969		455	221	18	2	171	867
1970		477	136	22	9	121	765
1971	5	405	467	26	8	219	1,130

A summary of the Zone 6 report says winter losses "may have reduced the zone population by 50 percent or more in 1971." I never could reconcile the figures with the lack of detailed information concerning winter kills, their exact locations and the number of deer lost. If winter kill was an important factor in the period, it certainly should have appeared as a category alongside cars and dogs.

Meanwhile, in Game Division Bulletin Number 6, Chester F. Banasiak, in the "Deer in Maine" section, wrote:

"Of the many recognized causes of deer mortalities, starvation is probably the last to be accepted as a possible cause of death by deer hunters. On the other hand, in an effort to get the point across that deer can and do starve in Maine, perhaps the subject has been over-emphasized on occasions. In either case, there continues to be confusion regarding the importance of starvation losses in the state."

The bulletin included figures from dead deer searches during 1955-56. In a total of 3,112 acres, five deer were described as victims of starvation; four were killed by predation, and the cause of death of 20 deer was listed as unknown.

Also included in the bulletin was a comparison of bobcat bounties and legal deer harvests from 1938 to 1958. Bobcat totals varied from a low of 211 in 1943 to a high of 810 in 1956, while legal deer registered varied from a low of 19,187 in 1939, to a high of 41,730 in 1951 (still a state record).

Banasiak noted that pending final analysis of the bobcat-deer relationship, it would appear that bobcats do not represent serious competition for hunters.

Coyotes undoubtedly depend on the snowshoe hare for food in all seasons. But it's my experience that deer, when available, become the prime target of coyotes as soon as snow covers the ground. And, as the number of coyotes increased, they began competing with bobcats for the same prey. During the winters from 1965 through 1981, I often noticed tracks of both animals following the same single deer or scouting the same deer run in a trodden yard.

On one occasion, in the town of Concord, I came upon the tracks of two bobcats and three coyotes trailing a single deer. The tracks were very fresh, on snow that had stopped falling less than an hour before I came upon them. I released Belle, one of the finest bobcat hounds I have hunted, certain she would segregate the scents and trail one of the bobcats. Despite tracking conditions complicated by the fact that several animals were traveling in the same direction, I had covered less than a mile when I saw where one bobcat had veered. Belle was following it. She eventually jumped the bobcat and treed it shortly thereafter. It was a 25-pound male.

The following day I returned out of curiosity to the same area. I intercepted the tracks of the three coyotes and the deer north of where I had left them to follow Belle the previous day. The second bobcat had not continued trailing the deer for some unknown reason. I came upon the remains of the deer within a mile. The coyotes had eaten practically all of it overnight.

Two of the largest attacks on deer I know of occurred in the town of Canaan in 1978 and at Caratunk a year later.

The Nelson brothers, Merle and Bertram, brought me to the Canaan kills in Sibley Bog. Eleven deer, eight of them adult does, had been killed and partly eaten. After examining the remains, I decided that a biologist from the Maine Fisheries-Wildlife Department should have the opportunity to view the mayhem.

I returned to the scene with regional biologist Gene Dumont. Six of the dead does were carrying twin fawns. Their general condition was good to excellent. There was some question whether the kills had been made by dogs. But after circling the bog with a snowmobile, I could find no trace of any dog-like animal having left the area. By 1975, coyotes had spread to the area and the deer population showed steep decline. I had found deer kills by coyotes in previous winters in the Burrill Woods and in the Morrill Pond areas, not far from Sibley Bog.

The Nelson brothers, sons of Guy Nelson, for years a respected warden and extremely knowledgeable outdoorsman, were trying at the time to reduce the coyote population by hunting. But they were finding out what others already had discovered: Coyotes travel long distances and, in Maine, are extremely difficult to intercept even when being chased by hounds.

Hoping to positively identify the animals responsible for the deer kills, the Nelsons set a trap near one of the dead deer on which considerable meat was left. The next day they found the remains of a fisher in it. There was little doubt that a coyote or coyotes had returned to the area, declined to feed on the deer after detecting the human scent but killed the fisher and ate most of it. The identity was further confirmed when urine was detected on the remains of the fisher, a coyote habit that is well-documented.

Stanley P. Young, noted naturalist who spent many years with the U.S. Biological Survey branch of wildlife research, wrote of similar behavior patterns as early as 1951:

"In my trapping experience, I have never successfully saved a trapped fox or bobcat from being killed by the coyote whenever a coyote visited a trapline ahead of me and found these animals in traps. Invariably the coyote tore them to shreds."

During the winter of 1978-79, deer kills by coyotes in an area from Pierce Pond to Caratunk and West Forks jumped in almost unbelievable fashion. Nine deer were driven to and killed on Wyman Lake during that winter, decimating what was left of a regional herd I estimated at 75 deer prior to the 1960s.

During February of 1980, when less than five inches of snow covered the same area, two more deer were driven to and killed at virtually the same spot by coyotes.

A few miles north of the area, Colin Bates, an experienced trapper, came upon two more deer kills while covering his beaver trapline. He also saw a single coyote drive an adult deer into the open water of Dead River at West Forks, the coyote giving up the chase although it had mangled both flanks of the deer.

Deer in all but extreme northwestern Maine probably were better able to escape predation during the winters of 1979-80 and 1980-81 than during any other period I remember. At no time were they seriously bogged down by deep snow and only in a few townships north and west of Greenville did the temperatures tumble to hazardous levels for deer.

Deer kills by coyotes nevertheless continued to spread. John Lemieux, a Dexter lumberman, reported six deer killed in February, 1981 in North Guilford. I found two more kills on Ross Lake where the deer had been driven onto the slippery surface by two or more coyotes.

In 1978, Henry Hilton, now with the Maine Fisheries-Wildlife Department, did his thesis at the University of Maine on two years of coyote research. A subsequent paper written for Academic Press, Inc., and published that same year, noted in part:

Among the more successful coyote trappers in Maine is Colin Bates of Caratunk shown with the catch of 16 he made during the fall-winter of 1979-80. This effort was hailed by Carroll York of West Forks and a key reason for a slight improvement in deer production in 1981. Bates says he has learned the hard way that trying to catch coyotes at the site of deer kills or next to a dead deer is a waste of time. Once human scent is noted, he believes, coyotes never return to a deer kill.

"Of the 17 deer killed in December through Feb. 13 (by coyotes) 13 were fawns while only six of the 21 killed in March and April were fawns. The mean age of males killed was 5 years and of females 7.5 years. Some of the adults exhibited abnormalities such as poor teeth, a badly healed broken leg and low marrow fat content in bones.

"The evidence that predation increased as the winter progressed may be attributed to increased vulnerability of wintering deer, their concentrated numbers and weakened condition (and) also to increased nutritional requirements of pregnant coyotes. Interestingly, it was during the late winter that groups of three and four coyotes were recorded most frequently during the tracking study. Whether these groups represented temporary social groups, organized to increase the efficiency of hunting large prey, is a question that should be considered in the future."

Because there is no evidence of a disastrous winter deer kill in Maine over the past century and because most of the dead deer found during the past 50 years were killed by something other than the elements, I am inclined to believe that predation, once by bobcats and in recent years also by coyotes, is among the most significant causes of the apparent decline in the number of deer.

I am not personally familiar with deer-coyote statistics in other states, but wildlife officials and practical observers have informed me that coyotes have had a profound effect on deer populations. In one state, Arizona, they have threatened the survival of antelope.

There is disagreement among scientific and non-scientific factions concerning the effect of the northeastern coyote on Maine deer. But they agree on one point: Deer very likely would have got along better had the new predator not invaded the state.

To Control or Not Control

The conflict concerning the true identity of the star of this book has been matched in intensity only by the divisive debate regarding the course of action, if any, wildlife managers should take to control it. It's no secret that there are differences of opinion among members of the Maine Fisheries-Wildlife Department and the University of Maine Cooperative Wildlife Research Unit. Officials everywhere are having a hard time reaching agreement on the question of how best to cope with the predation problem the northeastern coyote has brought to their states.

In fact, there is a widening breach between those who would control coyote populations and those who insist the animal should be left alone because it is not a threat to whitetail deer and has its place in the ecosystems.

On August 14, 1974, Dr. Voit B. Richens, then assistant professor of Wildlife Resources at the University of Maine Orono, as well as assistant leader of the Cooperative Wildlife Research Unit, made the following statement:

"It is my personal opinion that coyotes will have little effect on the whitetale deer herd. They will not kill a significant number as compared to the usual damage done by dogs."

Henry Hilton, assistant researcher assigned to study coyotes in 1973, wrote me: "You state there 'is sufficient evidence in Maine that coyotes kill deer in winter.' I agree, but that does not mean there is a problem. There is good evidence that coyotes have been in northwestern Aroostook County for at least 30 years and perhaps longer. There are still deer there."

Hilton is right, of course. The area still has a deer population, but most experienced sportsmen, myself included, estimate their numbers at less than half of the total there prior to the coyote invasion.

Other wildlife managers believe that predatory animals simply cannot be controlled. They describe the Maine coyote, or mongrel wolf, as elusive, smart and hard to catch. But I frequently encounter trappers with minimal experience who catch them rather handily. I know of one who in ten days in the Seboomook area caught 15. And a novice wildlife student once caught a female coyote twice in the same day, the second time after it had been collared with a radio transmitter.

In 1973 Richard B. Anderson, then director of the Maine Audubon Society, was among the critics to speak out when I wrote that coyotes were becoming a threat to deer. Counting himself among those who believe predatory animals cannot be effectively controlled by man, Anderson claimed there were more bobcats in Maine at that time than when the bounty went into effect. The speciousness of that assertion became evident two years later when the bounty, which ran from $2 when first introduced in 1836 to a peak of $20 in 1932-33, was revoked to lessen pressure of the popular predator.

Anderson, who later joined a state environmental agency, frankly was demonstrating his lack of knowledge of the bobcat situation. Monetary incentive, as has been proven many times, invariably adds great pressure to any harvestable wildlife resource and thereby contributes to a reduction in population. The truth of that can be discerned from a bobcat bounty payment chart for the years 1932 to 1936. The figures were provided by Archer L. Grover, deputy Maine Fish-Game commissioner.

The Maine bobcat bounty was initiated in 1836 and was $2 for each animal. The peak bounty of $20 was paid from November of 1932 to April of 1933 and resulted in a record catch of 960. Less than half the number of bobcats were bountied during the same period a year later and for many years thereafter.

For a number of years, from the 1940s until the late 1950s, pressure on bobcat populations diminished sharply because pelts were hardly worth skinning. During the early part of that period, members of the Warden Service who owned bobcat hounds were subsidized by the state to help control bobcats in a number of deer yards. The subsidy covered little more than the cost of dog food, but the program nevertheless did keep bobcat populations down in key deer yarding areas.

The 1960s marked the beginning of a tremendous rise in the price paid for bobcat pelts, from virtually nothing to peaks of $300. The incentive so increased trapping and hunting pressure that it was not unusual to find several parties ahead of me in areas where I had never encountered one in the previous 25 years.

Meanwhile, a new predator, the northeastern coyote, was moving into many of the ideal bobcat areas, competing for food and, as research was to show later, making survival for bobcats even more difficult. As a result, following revocation of the bounty, Maine in 1977-78 limited open seasons on trapping bobcats from mid-October to Dec. 1 and on hunting them from Dec. 1 to Feb. 28.

When the modern fur-bearing research projects began in 1978, it became obvious that control of any species, including Northeastern Coyotes, would not be a serious consideration of the Wildlife Research Unit. However, Commissioner Maynard F. Marsh, who retired in 1978, and his successor, Glenn H. Manuel, did approve coyote control programs in specific areas. And in 1983 the 111th Legislature finally recognized a need to act by funding a slightly broader control program.

There is substantial evidence that coyote populations can be effectively controlled. In 1951 Stanley P. Young and Hartley H. T. Jackson, then senior biologists with the Interior Department, described a successful experiment in their book, "The Clever Coyote." They wrote:

"In an attempt to restore deer herds in Duval County, Texas, from 1941-46 two areas approximating 67,000 and 92,000 acres were established. On these areas a combination of closed season on deer for five years, cooperation with the various oil companies, doubling of the warden forces, conservation teaching in the public schools together with predator control to the extent of removing a total of 4,142 predators, of which 3,851 were coyotes, showed a tentative increase of 357 percent in the deer population at the end of the four-year period."

The chapter on coyote control also noted that "a little time spent in April, May and June, in locating dens and destroying the young coyotes will save months of strenuous effort to rid the range of the predators after they have reached maturity."

Many of the areas which hold deer in Maine are smaller than the two in Texas where the control program took place. The terrain also is different, as are weather and seasonal range conditions.

It seems apparent that the best method of controlling Maine's northeastern coyote would be to locate dens and eliminate the puppies — rather than turn them loose after attaching radio transmitting collars to them.

Wildlife students conducting two Maine fur-bearing animal studies have been able to locate dens of northeastern coyotes so it is not an insurmountable task. Closer monitoring of deer yarding areas during average winter conditions and selective trapping of northeastern coyotes, if some are found, would be the next logical step.

No amount of promotion to encourage the hunting of northeastern coyote would, at this time, contribute much to controlling populations. It is possible to hunt them with hounds, much the same as hunting foxes or bobcats, but success has been spotty.

Telemetry tracking already has revealed how much ground coyotes can travel in a short period of time. A northeastern coyote equipped with a radio collar in Quebec was recovered a few weeks later at Squapan Lake in Maine, more than 100 miles away.

I was a member of a party that tried to overtake a pair of northeastern coyotes that traveled overnight from Benton to Brighton in fresh snow, a distance of 45 airline miles. The hounds still had not jumped them when picked up late in the day.

Hunters have bad success tracking and killing the animal. One party at Old Orchard Beach bagged a 40-pound male northeastern coyote shortly after their hounds jumped it in a rabbit thicket. But it still is the exception.

Jack Miner of Ontario was one of the greatest naturalists in recent times and remains the only person from North America to be knighted by British Royalty for his conservation efforts. Miner was a steadfast proponent of predator control, and his philosophy, at one time, was supported by Dr. Albert M. Day, chief of the U.S. Fish and Wildlife Service.

Among Miner's writings can be found the following: "God put the birds and animals here for man's use and for man's control. The same is true in regard to plant life. God made the weeds at the same time that he made the vegetables but it is man's job to destroy the weeds so that vegetables good for man can exist."

Miner experimented with several predator control programs, the first on this continent, and concluded that such controls helped produce more desirable wildlife species.

Today, the U.S. Fish and Wildlife Service believes it is unwise to "play one species of wildlife against the other." It is a vastly different policy than the one that reigned when Day was chief.

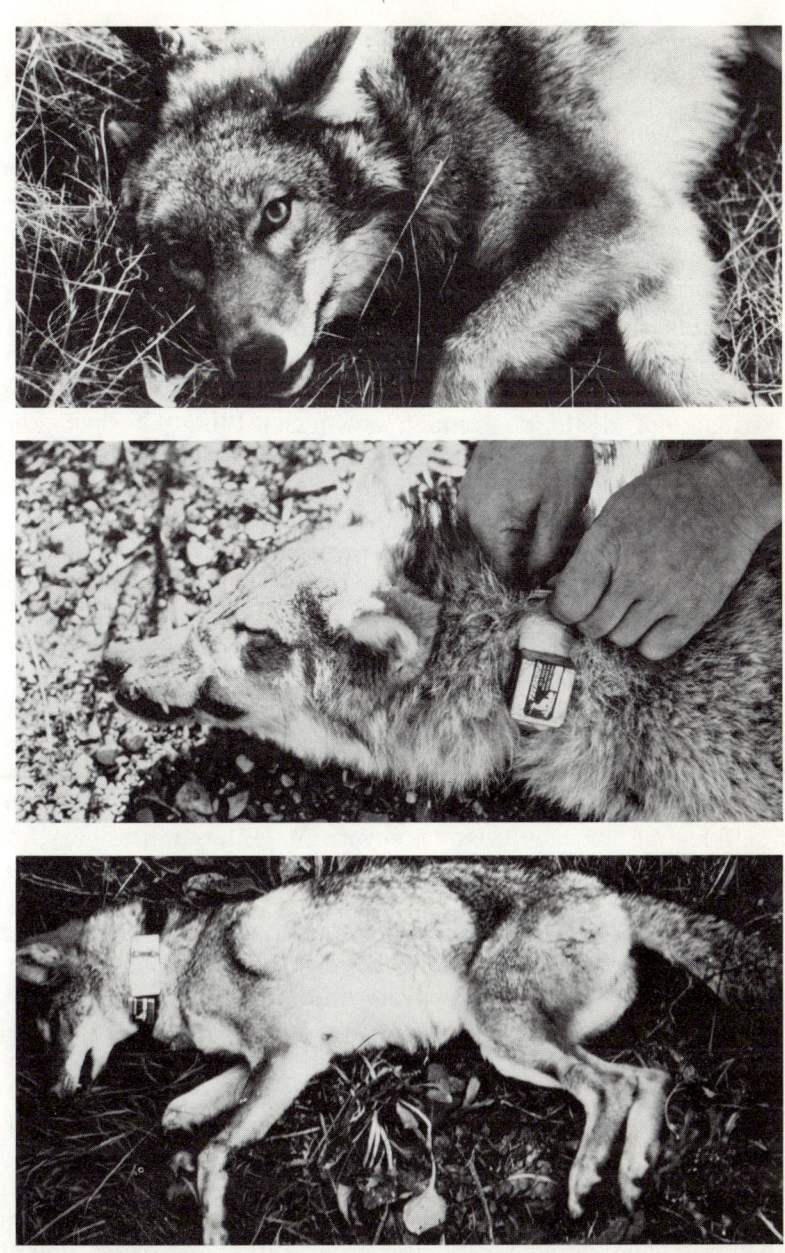

Trapping and equipping coyotes with radio collars to monitor their habits are part of the Maine research. This series of pictures show coyote after being caught and injected with tranquilizing drug then tested to make sure it is immobilized, equipped with collar and then recovering from the drug. (Photos courtesy Maine Wildlife Research Unit.)

I attended the annual meeting of the Outdoor Writers of America at North Bay, Ontario, in June, 1949 when Day endorsed the following resolution:

"Resolved that in view of the fact that many practical conservationists with extensive experience in the field view with alarm the tendency amongst some outdoor writers, likewise amongst Government officials, to accept with an attitude of complacency the undisturbed presence of predators in game habitat, the Outdoor Writers of America go on record sounding a word of alarm to such writers and conservation heads in areas where above conditions become noticeably apparent."

Day, in his address to the writers, declared, "We have to be realists not idealists. As much as we would like the coyote and fawn deer to lie down together, we know that only the coyote would get up and walk away from that siesta. We know there is no longer a true balance of nature in this country."

Day added that his department was succeeding in "whittling down the coyotes in the western range" through control programs.

The policies and functions of the federal agency Day once directed have changed considerably over the years. Its current policy on predator control often has been assailed by livestock and sheep herders. The new attitude was apparent when veteran federal wildlife agent Frank Gramlich of Maine was honored by the Interior Department on his retirement for his "defense of the northeastern coyote in Maine and alleviating public concern that its presence might seriously damage the deer herd."

In fairness to Gramlich, a personal friend and fellow bird hunter, it should be noted he believes the invasion of the northeastern coyote in Maine has been "unfortunate."

He could have added "unnecessary" for there is an example of a predatory animal that invaded Maine and was quickly controlled.

During the winter of 1948 Arthur G. Rogers, then a supervisor with the Maine Warden Service, reported that "strange, dog-like animals" were being seen in the Frankfort-Winterport area. Lawrence J. Guptill, a veteran trapper, had heard them howling, had found tracks and other signs, and killed one of them. It weighed 30 pounds and appeared to be a coyote. Guptill shot several more of the animals, several of which were identified as "coydogs" by University of Maine at Orono wildlife laboratory technicians.

These six coyote pups were found in a den in Waldo County in the early 1950s after John Guptill, center above, had caught a strange animal in a fox set. Warden Leon Gilpatrick, left, and the late Basil Closson, the latter a skilled trapper, helped to virtually eliminate the predators in the area. (Photo by Warden Supervisor Arthur G. Rogers, retired, of Waterville.)

In March of the following year Guptill found an active den of the animals and with the assistance of Wardens Leon Gilpatrick and Basil Closson captured six live pups. Given permission to try to raise them, Guptill soon discovered that it was not easy. They were vicious, he said later, and while he kept them until they were near adulthood, his efforts to tame and hand feed them proved futile. Each eventually bit him.

Rogers ordered killed any such pups found subsequently, both halting further population increases and reducing deer predation. Rogers explained the policy by noting that "the primary duty of a game department is to control depredations of predatory animals on game animals and to continually investigate all activities believed to be instigated by such creatures."

Rogers, who resides in Waterville, hasn't changed his opinion regarding predator control.

"It is either having such predators or deer," he contends. "Animals such as those and today's notheastern coyotes hunt

Coyote controllers reunited in this picture I took in October, 1981, were Leon Gilpatrick of Belfast, John Guptill, veteran trapper, and Arthur G. Rogers of Waterville. Gilpatrick was a warden, Rogers a warden supervisor, when Guptill caught a strange animal in a trap set for fox. When the animal was identified as a coyote, steps were taken immediately to control them. Guptill, who was employed by the Fisheries Wildlife Department, caught 31, led wardens to dens.

every day of the year, never stop. Allowing them to roam after finding their dens certainly is a negative approach to their proper control."

Rogers to this day feels Guptill and Closson solved the deer predation problem in the Frankfort area by virtually eliminating the "coydog" population.

On Nov. 8, 1981, Rogers, Gilpatrick and I visited Guptill. At 78 years of age, he was as sharp as the blade of the knife he used in skinning the many animals he has trapped. Surgery to remove eye cataracts and some unsteadiness in his walk had slowed him somewhat, but he brightened steadily as he recalled his experiences with coydogs.

Guptill also remembered his first contact with coyotes. He recalled that a neighbor had just lost four sheep by predation when he caught an unusual animal in a trap set for foxes on Fox Hill. Another neighbor, the first to see the animal, told Guptill he had a "yellow dog" in his trap.

"I knew right away this was no dog," Guptill said. "I also made sure it was not, in my personal opinion, a coydog. I noticed that unlike a dog; this animal and others that I caught later, had curved inside teeth, not straight ones like those of a domestic dog."

Warden Closson, an outstanding trapper who at the time was assigned to the Jackman region, was transferred to Waldo County to assist Guptill in reducing the population of the new predator.

"We both knew these animals were getting the deer down in these parts," Guptill related. "I noticed that in the snow or in mud it was easy to identify their tracks. The foot pad of the coyote is strawberry shaped, peaked in front, while those of a domestic dog are round.

"Nobody could outcatch Basil and me in trapping these coyotes. People in Augusta knew the problem but they simply would not listen to Rogers, Gilpatrick or Closson. We wanted an immediate, concentrated effort to stamp the coyote population completely out or reduce it to where the deer could recover."

Guptill and Closson trapped or caught in dens more than 30 coyotes and for a long period predation on deer and livestock in the general area was reduced.

Guptill carefully studied the habits of coyotes following his first catch. He discovered that when one took the track of a deer on snow, the others would fan from either side until the deer became exhausted.

"They always attacked from the flank," he said. "You can catch them in a trap near a deer kill if you make sure you approach the deer on the opposite side of where they are coming to the animal. You have to know your business to catch them on dry land."

Guptill was especially skeptical of the possibility that the state's deer population eventually will recover and become compatible with the northeastern coyote, an animal somewhat larger than the predator he trapped.

"Deer in Maine cannot stand the pressure of hunting, poaching and coyotes," Guptill replied. "There should have been an immediate incentive on the part of the Fisheries-Wildlife Department to prevent their increase in population and range. I think it could have been done."

Guptill and Rogers agreed that allowing northeastern coyote puppies to roam after their dens have been located is a "negative approach to their control."

The Maine Trappers Association also believes that coyotes can and should be controlled. Joe Baldwin of Garland, the group's president, proposed a new control policy to Commissioner Manuel in 1979. It called for a special coyote trapping season in the spring and others in the fall and late winter. Manuel was receptive to the proposal.

Baldwin, at a meeting of the Maine Deer Task Force in Bangor, called for "more cooperation among state and federal authorities and Maine trappers" in the effort to control coyotes. He noted that the "coyote is everyone's problem and I do not think we have time to sit back and wait. He is the supreme predator."

Manuel agreed.

The Fisheries-Wildlife department's recommended coyote control program actually was initiated in December of 1972 under Marsh. At the time wardens estimated the statewide coyote population at 125 to 550 animals. Marsh described the department's position as follows:

"Although recognizing that coyotes can and do kill deer and small livestock, the Department does not plan any massive coyote control programs which in other states have cost millions and have not been effective. The department recommends local control where they are causing particular problems but advises of the futility and expense of attempts to eradicate them.

On Nov. 9, 1979, Manuel issued a broader policy on coyote control. Prompted in part by the negligible success of a team of wardens selected to control "problem coyotes," it read:

"During the months of December, January, February, March and April department personnel and selected licensed trappers under the supervision of Warden Service personnel will be allowed to remove coyotes within and around wintering areas where there is evidence that coyotes are a threat to deer or other wildlife.

"Traps shall be tended at intervals of 24 hours in organized areas; 72 hours in unorganized areas. All coyotes except those taken by department personnel, shall be retained by the permittees. All other wildlife shall be released in the wild, or if dead in the trap, shall be forfeited to the department.

"Traps shall be placed at least 50 feet from any carcass or bait, except for water sets. Use of any traps with teeth on the jaws shall be unlawful.

"All wild animals taken or killed under authority of the permit shall be reported to the issuing warden within 12 hours of the killing. The report shall include the kind of animals, number and time and place of taking.

"The permit and a completed report of all animals shall be presented to the issuing warden within ten days of the last effective date of the permit or upon completion of trapping whichever comes first."

Manuel has told me he believes that predation by coyotes is a serious threat to deer and other animals in Maine. But even as he was announcing the new control program, the research unit was continuing to trap and release coyotes in two problem areas. A practical man with a background of potato farming, Manuel admitted to being disturbed because he could not reconcile saving coyotes for costly research on one hand and trying to control them on the other.

Few doubt that the deer in the research areas, both of them trouble spots, have been decimated by coyotes to a point where they are becoming rare.

There were other contradictions: Carl Ferguson, the predator control agent assigned to Maine by the U.S. Fish and Wildlife Service, had been effective in eliminating coyotes that were killing sheep in two areas. He was being paid by the same agency financing the fur-bearer research projects that allow coyotes to roam areas where deer were once plentiful.

Ferguson, who was primarily concerned with livestock predation, believed that eliminating coyote puppies was one of the most effective means of controlling the population. He noted that a dog trained to locate coyote dens was having great success in a western state. I wrote about his search for such a dog and he eventually found one he considered trainable. Unfortunately, a reduction in federal funds for predator control resulted in his transfer to another state.

Prior to Ferguson's departure, the wildlife service, with approval of the state's Department of Environmental Protection, resorted to use of the M-44 cyanide device to remove coyotes that were attacking sheep in four areas.

(In 1972 a federal executive order restricted the use of chemical toxicants both on federal lands and in federal programs to control livestock losses to coyotes and other predators. The order was amended in 1976 to allow use of the M-44, a spring-loaded device that dispenses sodium cyanide into the mouth of a predator or any animal that triggers it. It is partially buried and has a scented top to attract canids. A carbon monoxide gas cartridge fires when the cap is disturbed.)

The Maine project marked the first time the federal service had used such a device east of the Mississippi. It accounted for only one "probable" coyote in Maine between December, 1979 and July, 1980. Ferguson, who easily had more success taking coyotes by legtraps, defended the project, but members of the Sportsman's Alliance of Maine vociferously opposed it at a meeting held July 9, 1980.

George Easler of Dixfield, a veteran trapper, led the assault, contending the legtrap was a better tool for catching such animals. He joined the Maine Trappers Association in recommending a special trapping season — to follow the regular season on other fur-bearers — as a better means of controlling the predator.

All in all, the futility of Maine's coyote management program has done nothing but frustrate hunters who have seen considerable evidence that the northeastern coyote is a key factor in the decreasing population of whitetail deer in the northeast. They reason that deer are more valuable than coyotes and that one must go because the two are incompatible.

A study completed in 1981 by the University of Maine Orono Research Unit estimated the annual revenue from hunting in Maine at $70 million a year, excluding personal equipment such as rifles. More than $3 million in license fees goes directly to the Fisheries-Wildlife department, and more than 90 percent of the amount is directly related to deer hunting. Estimates place the value of a live deer in Maine at several hundred dollars compared with a harvestable return of $30 for each coyote.

The entire western portion of Maine — the area hardest hit by the coyote invasion — has felt the brunt of economic losses that resulted from lower deer populations the past six years. And while it is no secret that the scientific and practical factions of the Maine Department of Inland Fisheries and Wildlife seldom agree, they do share concern about the western zone's deer problem. However, they continue to disagree about both the causes of the decline and the kind of program that should be launched to rebuild the population.

Chester Banasiak, who heads the big-game research arm, steadfastly cites adverse winter conditions as the major factor for the decline, although he admits there has been some coyote predation.

Carroll York of West Forks, who heads the Maine Deer Task Force organized by the Sportsman's Alliance of Maine to study

Veteran fur-buyer Jim Day of Belgrade Lakes holds first northeastern coyote pelts brought to him. Largest measured nearly six feet in length, was multi-colored with considerable black. This was in February of 1975.

the problem, argues that deer held their own prior to the invasion of the "mystery mongrel."

Although York and Don Walker of Caratunk, a retired warden, failed because of a governor's veto, to inaugurate Maine's first antlered deer season in the troubled western zone in 1981, they succeeded in bringing the deer-coyote issue more into the public eye than ever before. The effort also led to approval of an abridged deer season in the zone as well as passage of legislation to protect doe deer in some areas.

There have been other "positive" developments.

The 111th Maine Legislature, through its Committee on Fisheries and Wildlife, authorized an appropriation of $85,000 to finance the newest statewide "Animal Damage Control" program. Legislators at the same time turned down several bills seeking bounties of $10 to $30 on northeastern coyotes.

The new program calls for establishing a full time coordinator and agents — trappers — who will be on call to kill troublesome coyotes and other predators, using any workable methods, including snares. The wage scale for agents is $6.50 an hour.

The Department of Fisheries and Wildlife advertised in several newspapers for agents and as of July 7, 1983, 30 persons had filed contracts with the department — 14 on a primary basis and 16 on standby.

Henry Hilton, a biologist, was named coordinator. As a research assistant with the Maine Cooperative Wildlife Unit at Orono in the 1970s, Hilton researched northeastern coyotes in the Big Black River area in Township 14 and Range 14. In a 1974 interview Hilton expressed doubt that the new predator in Maine was of the wolf family. Hilton transferred from the wildlife unit to the planning division of the department and was with the latter when named coordinator.

The new program will assess domestic and wild animal damage reports and determine the best means to control "trouble" predators.

The Legislature also passed an act to establish a night hunting season on coyotes from Jan. 1 to Feb. 28. It will be limited to shotguns and hunting must occur on snow or ice-covered areas between the hours of 9 p.m. and 4 a.m. Lights and special calls are permitted to bring coyotes to stands. Free permits will be issued by the Fisheries-Wildlife Department. The Sportsman's Alliance of Maine has described the programs as "too little too late."

Meanwhile, proposals for selective, early trapping of the coyote, outlined at public hearings during the summer of 1983, drew stiff opposition from members of bear, raccoon, bird and beagle clubs as well as individual hunters who use dogs. The proposals emanated from trappers who contend trapping from Oct. 10 to 25 would be an effective way to reduce the coyote population.

Dog owners counter that an early October season would place their hounds, bird dogs and retrievers in range of the land sets, which would be the only trapping method allowed.

I continue to believe an effective method of controlling the animal in my home state of Maine has yet to be devised, although finding dens and eliminating litters — a method recommended by the U.S. Fish and Wildlife Service in the 1940s — appears to have considerable promise. Robert W. Boettger, chief of Maine's Game Division, vehemently opposed the introduction of "true" wolves in Maine when it was suggested by a team of federal and midwestern states wildlife technicians. Boettger turned down a proposal to establish three wolf areas, noting that the animal's natural prey consists of white-tailed deer, moose and beaver.

Boettger said the Maine department was "sticking to its longstanding policy of not supporting the introduction of any species of fish or wildlife until there is conclusive evidence that populations of existing native species will not be adversely affected."

During the National Retrieving Dog Championship trials held in the Waterville, Maine area in June, 1980, I was fortunate to meet James L. Mauney of Indian, Alaska, who had traveled all that distance to enter his labrador in the competition.

One of the more significant features of our conversations was about the control of predators.

Mauney declared he was "positively sure" that control of predators indeed is possible today.

"We have a public sentiment problem with wolves in Alaska," Mauney said, "but when the situation boils down to whether the wolves are to be favored over the moose and caribou, the eatables have the wide edge."

Mauney, at that time, had been a biologist with the U.S. Fish and Wildlife Service in Alaska for 14 years. He asserted that with the means available today to wildlife managers predator control can be effective and thorough.

Maintaining good deer yards is the topic being discussed in picture, above, taken at the Kennebago River wildlife management area. Left to right, are "Skip" Davenport of Oquossoc, Carrol York of West Forks and biologist Mark Stadler. Davenport, a veteran trapper, and York, a professional forester, have been strong on good woods practices and predator control in an effort to rebuild the deer herd. York headed the first Maine Deer Task Force organized in Maine.

Predator control factions, in fact, were making progress in several states. Minnesota's Wildlife Division succeeded in having the timber wolf removed from the endangered species list about the same time the Arizona Game and Fish Department embarked on a coyote control program to curb the loss of antelope fawns.

Early in January of 1983 the Alberta (Canada) government announced a program aimed at decreasing an "inflated wolf population." It called for extensive trapping and poisoning, the latter always subject to considerable opposition in any Maine predator or rabies control program.

Alberta Fish and Wildlife officials estimated the wolf population had risen to 5,000 — an increase of 2,000 during the past decade — and noted that many ranchers and hunters had been complaining about increased wolf attacks on domestic animals and competition for big game.

The government's long-term strategy includes keeping the wolf population between 4,000 and 5,000, more effective monitoring, promoting an annual trapper harvest of 30 percent of the population and liberalizing hunting regulations. The program, except for poisoning, is strikingly similar to the relatively ineffective Maine plan outlined in 1979 by Commissioner Manuel.

Alaska, Minnesota, Arizona, Wisconsin and Michigan are among states that have problems convincing the public that predator control sometimes is necessary.

In 1982, Arizona nevertheless staged helicopter assaults on coyotes hoping to kill up to 300 of them on the Anderson Mesa. State wildlife officials said they had two choices: do nothing and allow coyotes to decimate the antelope, or take strong steps to reduce coyote numbers in selected problem areas. They chose the latter.

In Minnesota private hunting clubs have contributed as much to the control of coyotes as any medium. But the big hunts by organized clubs have come under attack in recent years — from urbanites who probably have never seen a deer killed by a predator.

Television has contributed a great deal to the sentiment against predator control with documentaries purporting to show that all wild animals can live together harmoniously. It would be impractical — perhaps impossible — to show what actually happens in an unfenced area populated by whitetail deer, bobcats, wolves and northeastern coyotes.

If the only law were "survival of the fittest," the gentle deer would be sorely lacking equal protection.

Reggie Vigue of Fairfield and 46-pound coyote he killed near his home on November 23, 1981.

How Dangerous To People

Does the northeastern coyote pose a threat to humans?

In California, a child was killed by coyotes, another maimed, and joggers were placed on alert if they ventured out at night.

In Maine, there have been at least three attacks on humans by coyotes, one of which may have been provoked, the others initiated by the animals for no obvious reason.

On February 23, 1980, Ronnie Thomas, a Waterville city parks employee who has a camp on Indian Pond, The Forks, came upon two coyotes that had a deer down on the ice. When he attempted to drive them away with his snowmobile, they chose to protect their kill, baring teeth, growling and refusing to leave.

Thomas continued to his camp to obtain a gun. He returned in time to watch them lope toward the woods and disappear. Had they eaten their fill or were they instinctively aware that Thomas would be armed? It's impossible to say, but Thomas believes that coyotes are aware of and afraid of guns. On previous occasions when he had seen coyotes and was armed, they had dashed quickly into the woods.

On August 25, 1981, Hazen Hall of Amity, a farmer-woodsman, went to his woodlot to do some thinning. As he was trying to start his chain saw, four coyotes appeared in the clearing where he had parked his truck.

Hall tried to drive them off but they challenged him. Climbing on the hood of the truck as one of the coyotes grabbed his pantleg, Hall used his chain saw to ward off the attacker and then threw the saw at the animals. They retreated just enough for him to reach for the M1 rifle in the cab of his truck and kill one of them.

Hall was not injured, but his pantleg was indeed ripped, according to Fisheries-Wildlife Commissioner Glenn H. Manuel who has known the Amity resident for many years and would vouch for his credibility.

The dead coyote was sent to the University of Maine, Orono, laboratory for examination. Tests revealed it was not rabid.

The coyote attack on Hall certainly was unprovoked. The incident involving Thomas was somewhat different in that he had challenged the animals to the right of possession of their kill.

On Sunday, November 15, 1981, Lawrence Kimball told Constable Manton Emerson that two animals, each weighing about 35 pounds, attacked him near his home on Northern Avenue in Farmingdale, which is located between Augusta and Gardiner.

Kimball told Emerson he attempted to scare off the animals with a stove pipe but eventually had to seek shelter in his garage. While Kimball suffered no physical injury, he was greatly upset by the encounter, said Emerson, who warned residents of the community to stay away from any strange animals they might observe.

According to Emerson, reports of coyotes roaming within the town limits had been received prior to Kimball's experience. Leroy Shea, another Farmingdale resident, said he had heard them yipping at his front door.

In "Coyotes In Our Family," an article by Warden Rodney D. Sirois of St. Pamphile, Quebec, that appeared in the Maine Fish and Wildlife magazine in the fall of 1979, Sirois related how two coyotes he was raising brought "happiness, pure joy and terror" into the life of his family.

Sirois, a veteran warden with the Maine Department of Fisheries and Wildlife, became interested in coyotes when they first were reported in his border district. In the spring of 1975, when Henry Hilton, a biologist, was concentrating on coyotes for his Masters degree, Sirois and Warden Inspector Oral Page, found a coyote den with seven young. Five were flown to the University of Colorado for a behavior study and Sirois kept the other two, a male and a female, hoping to raise them for research purposes.

The coyotes were two years old when terror struck. The male then weighed 40 pounds, the female a few pounds less.

During February, 1977, Sirois was called to Southern Maine on special assignment. His wife, Judy, took over feeding the coyotes. During one of the feeding sessions, the female coyote, Princess, in season and more aggressive than usual, slipped out of the pen, grabbed the Sirois' youngest son Guy, not yet two years old, inflicting wounds in his face that required 22 stitches.

This male coyote pup was one of two raised by Warden Rod Sirois of St. Pamphille, P.Q., who has done a long-range study of the predators in the St. John River regions. (Photo by Henry Hilton.)

"Judy," Sirois wrote, "with the fighting fury of a mother defending her young, pulled Princess off. While Judy was screaming for someone to help, she sheltered Guy's torn and bleeding face in her arms. Princess then attacked Clem, five, biting him on the back of the head as he ran for the house. Judy was able to ward off further attacks."

Clem's wounds required 15 stitches. "It was," Sirois wrote, "with a lot of sorrow that I dispatched both of the animals." He believed the attack on the children was mainly due to jealousy.

"Princess did not intend to kill Guy or Clem," Sirois wrote, "only to put them in their places and establish her dominance. Coyotes often grab with their teeth and shake one another violently to establish order. A child's skin is far too tender to withstand the sharp teeth of a coyote. We fully realize that Princess was capable of crushing Guy's or Clem's skull if she had intended to kill them.

"By sharing our home with Tonka and Princess, we learned more about coyotes than their mere physical needs. We learned that the emotions shown by them were similar to those displayed by man's best friend, the dog. We learned about our responsibility to not interfere with wild animals."

Sirois clearly brings out the varied sentiment concerning coyotes. Despite the experience involving his family, he writes, "we learned that coyotes belong in the woods and have a right to live there, fulfilling their natural predator-prey relationship within the wildlife community. In our lifetime we have witnessed the migration of an animal into the Maine woods whose importance is not yet fully understood."

Sirois' evaluation of the coyote's place in Maine isn't unanimously accepted by fellow wardens and many others who have contacted me with reports of incidents that do not place the animal on a pedestal.

Henry McKenna of Milton Plantation, for example, wished the coyotes had never come to Maine. He lost his pet beagle hound to coyotes that had been feeding on discarded hens from a poultry plant near his home.

McKenna, an experienced trapper, searched for the beagle when it did not return from an exercise run. There was snow on the ground, allowing him to track the dog. The tracks suddenly multiplied, a sign that was to bode ill for McKenna's pet.

"My beagle was still alive when I came upon him. He had been slashed to bits from head to shoulders. We had to put him away. From the tracks I would say that a pack of four or five coyotes had done him in," McKenna said.

Milton Plantation is in an area that spawned reports of coyote predation during the early 1970s. They included unexplained disappearances of cats and dogs and a steady decline in deer.

In the December 23, 1981, issue of the *Central Maine Sentinel*, Stephen Collins, a correspondent, reported that Gordon Pepper of the Penney Road, Belgrade, had lost two young beagles and a newborn calf to coyote attacks.

"'Three of the Pepper beagles were in a field when a couple of the wild animals came out of the edge of the woods,' Pepper related. 'Two of the dogs were just over a year old, saw the coyotes and chased them back into the wooded area where we later found the beagles dead. The mother of the two pups did not give chase and was not attacked."

The article continued: "During the first week of December, one of the Pepper cows gave birth in a field away from the house and after the season's first snowfall hit, the coyotes moved in and killed the calf.

"Pepper also said there is a woman who lives nearby who is missing some of her cats and he's pretty sure they've met the same fate. He said he thinks that the coyotes hang around farms because they know that there is always some kind of food around.

"'They did clean the woodchucks out, but that's the only good they've done,' said Pepper. An avid rabbit hunter, Pepper has suffered double jeopardy. In addition to losing two beagles that were already running rabbits, he said the rabbit population has been decimated as well.

"'I've shot as many as 40 in a season in one spot,' he said, adding that now there are fewer and fewer despite plenty of feed and cover for them.

"A neighboring farmer, Fred Perkins, said that there have been no deer around to speak of since the coyotes moved in. He hasn't lost any animals from his farm to the predators, but he's seen them moving in right behind his cows and reports that three coyotes have been killed around his place.

"Pepper said that two of the dead coyotes have weighed in at 44 and 45 pounds and that he's sure there are bigger ones still at large."

Other incidents involving coyotes and domestic animals have been reported to me over the years, but the ones mentioned here are typical.

John and Danny Longley with 54-pound coyote bagged near their Anson home on September 9, 1975.

    Maine has long enjoyed an enviable reputation based on the premise that there is nothing in its fields, woods and waters that can seriously harm a human. I have often noted this feature in various writings with some pride.

    The lack of poisonous snakes (probably nonexistent in any part of the state) and wildlife that would rather shy from humans than challenge them has made Maine's outdoors attractive to tourists, campers and hikers as well as fishermen and hunters.

    There are some veteran wardens, both in forestry and wildlife, and woodsmen who fear that era may be over. Retired

Warden Supervisor Arthur G. Rogers of Waterville, whose personal experiences with predators are extensive, points out that the large size of the coyote in this state should be sufficient to consider the animal dangerous to human safety.

Rogers, who maintains contact with farmers, sportsmen and active wardens, says he is particularly bothered by reports of coyotes watching farmers working in their fields.

"They're becoming accustomed to the Maine scene," Rogers notes, "and becoming bolder. I dread to think what a pair of them could do to a child."

Biologists generally continue to discount any possibility of these animals becoming dangerous, insisting they will continue to avoid contact with humans.

I have spent many days and nights in the Maine woods under almost every variety of conditions. Never have I been concerned

Jack Lasalle of Pittsfield bagged this 40-pound coyote while deer hunting.

that any living thing, except man, might harm me or my dogs. As I accumulate information about coyotes, I can't help but wonder if the new predator that has invaded every corner of the state will some day prey on my "peace of mind."

Tracks of northeastern coyotes above in Deadwater area following a ten-inch snowfall. They measured four inches wide, five inches long including the tip of the two longest or front toenails, the latter tell-tale evidence of what made them. Toenails seldom show in bobcat or Canada lynx tracks.

The People Speak

Few wild animals have aroused such public interest as the invader that has been scientifically identified as the northeastern coyote. The reception accorded the animal by readers of my daily "Sportsmen Say" column has been mixed. But those who contribute most financially to Fisheries-Wildlife management, the hunters and sportsmen who buy licenses and permits, want the predator controlled and more emphasis on improving the deer population and its habitat.

Space simply does not permit publishing every comment, oral and written, I have received since I first reported the appearance of the animal. A selection, however, indicates the general sentiment regarding the mystery mongrel of Maine and New England.

One morning I was awakened at 6:30 a.m. by a woman who would not identify herself. She was incensed, furious, and said she had just finished reading a column referring to a multiple deer kill by coyotes in a Dexter woodlot.

"You have no right," she shrieked, "to write the way you do about the coyote. This is a nice, peaceful animal that has a place in the ecosystem. You should be ashamed to write anything like that. I want you to leave that poor, harmless animal alone." With that she slammed down the phone.

Included in the mail I have received was a fairly good cartoon depicting an armed coyote aiming its rifle at my head.

My fairness, which has kept me in the newspaper field 53 years, was questioned several times, but I also received plenty of support.

Marvin W. Hupper of the Parkman Hill Road, South Solon, wrote: "I've been reading your articles on coyotes with interest but have questioned how harmful they are to deer. This morning on my daily jog I came over a hill and saw two adult deer ahead. They acted very nervous and agitated. As I approached, one ran right into the woods and the other toward a large field. A large coyote, the first I have seen in the wild, was in the field and gave chase. I yelled several times but the coyote gave no indication that it heard me. The last I saw of him he had chased the deer into the woods."

That incident occurred on July 24, 1981, and the visual evidence obviously changed some of Mr. Hupper's thinking.

Earlier that same month, James Datsis, an official with the Maine Department of Human Services and a veteran trout fisherman, was casting at a small pond in upper Somerset County when he saw a doe crash out of the woods into the water.

I have fished with Datsis many times and we had not seen a deer at that pond for seven years. Prior to the invasion of coyotes it was not uncommon to have six to a dozen watch us on a summer day while we fished for trout.

The deer was blowing and bleating, and ran up and down the shoreline several times, stopping briefly to look back into the woods and stomp her front feet.

"I felt convinced she had been chased by one or more coyotes," Datsis later related, "and that she most likely was trying to protect her fawn or fawns.

"Having seen many signs of coyotes in the area for the past several years and found evidence of deer kills, there could be little doubt that her panic was predatory related. She remained in the water for half an hour before sneaking back into the woods."

Lloyd Niles of Stratton, among the keenest of wildlife observers in Maine, had a serious bout with coyotes while trying to raise sheep. His losses to them, he complained, were never compensated through damage claims. He became rightly incensed when questions were raised as to what animal was raiding his flock.

While driving on Route 27 one day, he saw a doe, bleeding profusely from her hindquarters, lumber across the road. Seconds later a large coyote bounded on the deer's track. Unarmed at the time, Niles drove to his home, got a rifle, and returned to where he had witnessed the chase.

Niles had little difficulty following the blood trail of the deer. She was dying when he overtook her but the coyote had departed, having scented and heard Niles coming. Niles humanely disposed of the deer.

"It took that incident and a deer kill to convince my doubters that I knew what was killing my sheep," he told me later, adding he "rued the day coyotes came to Maine."

The attitude of most wildlife managers and researchers in Maine has been that the coyote is here and we must live with it. It may be the reason why the animal is defended by persons such as the woman who challenged my right to publish anything that might sound detrimental to predators.

For each coyote defender, however, there have been a dozen readers calling for some means of control, arguing that coyotes and deer cannot co-exist in a state like Maine. The tremendous increase in coyotes during the past 15 years is a signal to them that the proportion of deer to coyotes is out of whack.

Robert Clark of Jefferson has lost more sheep to coyote predation than any other Maine resident. He became convinced of what was raiding his flocks when he came upon a coyote on a fresh kill. Clark had reported 50 lambs killed by coyotes only to have a member of the Fisheries-Wildlife department testify at a public gathering in Boothbay Harbor, about 20 miles from Jefferson, that coyotes were not a problem in that particular area.

Clark didn't just watch his sheep vanish. He also killed an adult coyote while it was in the process of eating one of the sheep. Had he not done so, he likely would have had difficulty convincing livestock damage investigators that coyotes were to blame for his losses.

Carl Ferguson, an agent of the U.S. Fish and Wildlife Service stationed in Maine at the time, was given the task of trying to control the predators raiding the Clark sheep. The assignment led to an important discovery.

While tracking a coyote, he found that it had treed a fisher, the most valuable fur-bearing animal in Maine. Other coyote tracks nearby led to two other fishers that had been treed. It was the first visual evidence found in Maine confirming that coyotes did indeed chase animals larger than squirrels.

The majority of letters I have received deplore the invasion of the northeastern coyote, its rapid increase in range and the lack of a bona fide attempt to control its population.

Herbert Foster of Farmington, one of the most successful fisher trappers in Maine, called attention to predation on deer and small fur-bearers shortly after the coyote made its first appearance. Foster turned 81 on Jan. 8, 1983, and used the occasion to renew his personal assault on modern wildlife managers who "continue to be unreceptive to any ideas, advice or suggestions from any exterior source."

He was especially critical of one research effort in the Pierce Pond area of Somerset County, saying the project "stands as a monument to anti-conservation . . ." He explained that it "involved the release of over 40 coyotes in what once was the best deer range in Maine after equipping them with radio transmitting collars.

"Every thoughtful sportsmen having cognizance of this breach of our faith in the wildlife managers," said Foster, "must ponder the miniscule potential value of any information so obtained compared to the damage these creatures and their progeny will inflict upon the highly more desirable species."

As far back as Dec. 10, 1973, Robert Boilard of Biddeford wrote me to note the decline of deer in southern Maine. He called for immediate protection of does and said a control program to stem the growing population of northeastern coyotes should be a priority of the Department of Fisheries and Wildlife.

Boilard not only is a leading "practical" authority on salt water fishing but is well informed about statewide wildlife conditions.

"Otherwise," Boilard added, "we will have no deer season at all . . . and, worse, no deer."

Ten years later, reduction of deer hunting seasons, protection of does and a possible new type of northeastern coyote control loom as possibilities.

Lionel Caron is a retired Maine forest warden who resides on the shores of Chemquasasamticook (Ross) Lake. His first recollection of a wolf-like animal being sighted in Maine goes back about 56 years — the same time I first witnessed the impact the creatures can have.

Fresh out of high school, I drove a Model T Ford from Waterville, Maine to St. Pamphille, Quebec, to visit Albert Thibodeau, a Maine forest warden and good friend. I never expected then that an incident there would become part of a book I would write so many years later.

While my visit primarily was to fish for trout in such waters as the Big and Little Black rivers, I was "drafted" to play on the "visiting" baseball team against the hometown nine.

During one of the Sunday games Thibodeau's dog Major, an extremely intelligent Airedale, wandered from the ball park. When the dog failed to return, we launched a search and discovered that a farmer had shot him as he approached the farmer's flock of sheep.

A week later it was discovered that the farmer was losing

sheep not to dogs but to a "loupcervier," as the wolf was commonly known to French Canadians.

According to Caron, two of the "wolves" were eventually killed. The Quebec Wildlife Laboratory identified one as a "brush wolf" and the other as having mixed genes. An American laboratory that also examined one of the mongrels determined that it was part coyote and part domestic dog.

Caron was forest supervisor in the St. John district when he retired. He built his retirement home a short distance from the camps owned by the Guy Gannett Publishing Co., which I have supervised for many years.

It was when I asked Caron for his opinion about the effect of the northeastern coyote on Maine deer that he recalled the incident at St. Pamphille as well as another concerning the appearance of "wolves" about the same time on an island in the St. John. It has been known as Wolf Island ever since.

Caron is a knowledgeable, practical outdoorsman. Nobody is more familiar with the upper St. John region than the retired warden. And while he believes the new canid cannot be entirely blamed for all deer declines, he sees a need for some control of the animal where it is a possible threat.

While I was checking the company camps in February, 1980, Caron came over for a chat and we eventually moved into the subject of coyotes. He had just found two deer kills by a pack despite the open conditions of that winter.

"The deer were driven onto glare ice," he informed me, "and that was their demise."

Caron does not subscribe to the belief that northeastern coyotes are difficult to trap. He approves of issuing special trapping permits to responsible persons whenever control is needed in certain areas.

Blaine Lambert, a member of the Maine Deer Task Force, has trapped northern Aroostook County for years. He has seen evidence of the northeastern coyote stalking beavers, when conditions favored such tactics. He also has found the remains of young beavers he feels sure were killed by the predators.

Dr. Lowell E. Barnes of Hiram, an octogenarian, began in 1963, he told me, to alert as many people as possible to the decimation of the deer herd by coyotes. Barnes contends that too many Maine citizens have been "misled and brainwashed into believing that this animal is not the greatest predator of deer ever to exist within our forests."

Barnes is the son of a Maine guide and a nature-oriented mother. Both, he notes, "took to the woods with love and respect for all living things."

Barnes insists that the only persons totally aware of the predation by these canids are those who get out of their armchairs in winter, visit the deer areas and see for themselves.

"There are many misled people within the confines of warm homes that have no knowledge of what has happened in our forests," Barnes wrote in one of his letters to me.

"I have only one wish in mind," Barnes added, "and that is for all persons desirous of maintaining a wealth of creatures in our forests to band together and over-ride the material foisted upon us by book-educated, armchair planners of our fisheries and wildlife who have done more to cause their demise than enhance them."

E. H. Smith of Wells has an entirely different attitude toward the northeastern coyote. The head of Smith Enterprises believes the animal, which he prefers to identify as "brush wolf," is "surely no threat to anyone but the hogs that covet everything for themselves."

Smith was running a kennel at the time that he wrote me, breeding cross canines of wolf-dog genes and publishing a newsletter entitled "Age of Wolves." He also was in the process of publishing a book about the animals.

"Even if the brush wolves killed four to five percent of the total annual deer kill," Smith wrote, "this is a very small number. I suggest that we list stopping domestic dogs and poaching first."

Many Maine residents with years of outdoor experience have written me along similar lines.

Chester Banasiak, Maine's big game research leader, does not consider the coyote as much a contributing factor to deer declines as long-term adverse winter severity and modern lumbering practices.

In a report prepared in February, 1979, Banasiak outlined deer management alternatives for western Maine. The following was on predation:

"Predators in Maine, other than dogs, capable of killing deer include the bobcat, coyote, bear and fisher. Of these, the coyote currently remains abundant enough for concern.

"Spread of the coyote in Maine has been in a west to east direction and coyote populations were present in western Maine prior to the decline of deer in the early 1960s and 1970s. However, attributing the deer population decline in western Maine solely to the effects of predation by coyotes does not logically follow.

"The decrease in deer numbers occurred in eastern Maine as well as in New Brunswick and Nova Scotia where coyotes were absent or rare. This does not imply that coyotes are not contributing to the continued depression of deer populations in western Maine."

Robert W. Boettger, chief of the Maine Game Division, has repeatedly acknowledged the increase of coyotes but also does not believe the predator is the more serious of the adverse factors on the deer population.

"We are wholly aware of the presence of the coyote," Boettger has told me, "but we feel we must live with it."

Kenneth Robinson of Savage Hill, Concord, has been a successful cattleman and farmer for many years. He owns land bordering an extensive tract of ideal wildlife habitat. An ardent outdoorsman, he has watched deer decline steadily as coyotes increased in that specific region.

I have hunted bobcats in the area for nearly 50 years. It would be ideal for research on the effects of coyote predation. Before coyotes populated the area, I often ran into herds of 25 to 50 deer while tracking bobcats. During the past 20 years, their numbers have dwindled to a point where it has become a rarity to see even two or three deer while covering the area.

"I think it is a shame," Robinson told me, "to witness the failure of our wildlife managers to accept the situation without genuine effort to stem the tide of predation on deer."

Even people who want to see the coyote have a place in the ecosystem fear that unless there is some weeding of the undesirables (coyotes), there will be no opportunity to harvest the desirables (deer). To make his point Robinson compares coyotes and deer to weeds and vegetables. They are not, in his opinion, totally compatible.

Earl Shaw of Unity, a bobcat hunter, is among those concerned about the effects coyotes are having on wildcats.

Four winters ago Shaw found eleven deer killed by coyotes in Unity Plantation. He notified the district warden who in turn informed regional biologists.

"I showed them the deer kills," Shaw told me later, "but their attitude was quite indifferent. Nothing ever happened concern-

Among the first Maine residents to watch the decline of deer following the invasions of coyotes was Kenneth Robinson of Concord who is shown above with a 48-pound coyote he killed in his field. Twenty years ago 50 to 100 deer wintered near his home and I often chatted with him while bobcat hunting. After the coyotes moved in, it became difficult to follow tracks of bobcats and dogs so mixed were they with those of coyotes. Meanwhile, 70 percent of the long-term average wintering deer herd vanished.

ing the situation. Since then I have felt that there is not much sense in telling the Fisheries-Wildlife Department anything."

Shaw, an experienced bobcat hunter, also is convinced that coyotes are giving bobcats a hard time.

"I already had noted that deer were bunched up more where coyotes were active. When we found large bobcats following the same pattern, and their numbers decidedly down, I became convinced that coyotes indeed were raising hell with the bobcat population," Shaw told me.

"But we've been seeing fewer deer every winter," Shaw noted. "The population in Washington County, where coyotes are prevalent, is way down in my humble opinion."

The following letter from William Pearson of Wellington reflects the attitude of people who believe the coyote has a place in Maine's wildlife family.

"In your column, you state that Earl Shaw of Unity believes (and apparently you do also) that not only are the coyotes of Maine raising havoc with the deer of the state 'but with most of the state's native wild animals and birds.'

"Have you forgotten, Mr. Letourneau, that the northeastern coyote, albeit a somewhat different species than its predecessor, the wolf, was a native of this region for centuries before our European ancestors came to know America? It was only when our predecessors, mostly through their fear of this animal, wiped out the majority of the wolves living at the time and driving the remaining few to less hostile places, that these animals became 'extinct' in the northeast. These animals, whether they be wolves or coyotes, fill a necessary ecological niche here in the Maine woods, thereby making them an important and viable character in the continuation and, indeed, in the preservation of all the wild animals of the state.

"I respect you for your knowledge of the wild animals of this state, Mr. Letourneau. It is my opinion though that you do not take into consideration the fact that the 'scheme' of nature does not include man on the scale he influences the world around him today. Many animals have been almost wiped out of existence here in the Maine woods within the last century or so. The moose, fisher, bobcat, beaver and several others are just some of the animals that have been overly hunted and trapped and are only now making a comeback. The northeastern coyote is only one of many to reappear in the woods, in its case filling the void left by the demise of its predecessor, the wolf. I do not doubt that coyotes kill several deer a year and even more livestock but this does not make the coyote a 'criminal' of the forest. The coyote is only playing out its part in the life cycle of nature. Its depredation upon other wildlife remains insignificant in comparison with the number of deer and other wildlife taken by hunters each year.

"I do not advocate an end to hunting (except spring bear hunting season) but I do believe that coyotes should not take very much of the blame for the reduction in any game animal population, whether it be deer, bobcat, fisher or whatever.

"Deer and coyotes, or wolves if you wish, have co-habited for a good many years and I expect they could do so for a good many more to come. Life and death is an everyday event in the wilds, as I'm sure you know. One animal dies so another can live. It's like a tree that dies, it falls to the forest floor, and then nurtures many other trees as they develop. Though the tree that fell was a fir, a maple grew out of its decaying trunk but a tree nonetheless. The same is true in the animal world; one animal dies or is killed, another feeds on its carcass, that one lives until its day comes to be the food of some other animal. There's nothing cruel about it; that's the way it's meant to be by whoever or whatever may have deemed it so.

"What all this amounts to is that I do not consider the coyote a 'liability.' Indeed it is more like an asset. To myself the return of the coyote signals that nature is on the road to recovery from the decimation it suffered in years past, and since we now realize, contrary to our forefathers beliefs, that nature and its resources are indeed limited, perhaps we will better manage them this second time around. To me that means not wiping out any particular species, whether that species be coyotes or fir trees."

I find as I near the conclusion of this book, that future management of the coyote in Maine appears to have reached an impasse, certainly as it relates to the white-tailed deer.

As of mid-January, 1982, Maine was in the middle of a winter as severe as any since the early 1960s when I first found evidence of deer predation by the northeastern coyote. Snow depths ranged from 26 inches in central areas to 40 inches in many northern areas.

I telephoned Walter C. "Skeet" Davenport of Rangeley at that point to confirm the weight of the coyote Terry Richardson of Gorham had caught (it was a record 76 pounds for Maine coyotes) and found him greatly concerned about the deer situation in his area.

While setting and checking his beaver traps, Davenport, a

member of the Maine Deer Task Force, said he had noted that the coyotes were returning to areas that still held a few deer.

"I am afraid," Davenport said, "that what deer are left in this part of Maine will have a difficult time to survive this winter."

Davenport, who often has pointed out that the demise of deer is not entirely related to the invasion of coyotes, told me that the added menace of coyotes at this point in time will delay the comeback of the deer. "They just can't stand all the adversities," Davenport asserted.

Davenport noted that while about three feet of snow covered the area with which he is thoroughly familiar, there were crust layers which, combined with the texture of snow, formed a good base for snowshoeing. Several deer were using his "floats" or packed snowshoe trails, Davenport told me, to reach cutting where food was available to them. One deer, a lone buck, followed one trail nearly four miles to reach such a place. While the area is only one of the many places in Maine where deer face similar problems, it is typical of what is happening.

"This past fall, the coyotes kept the deer on the move and stirred up in the Gebung Woods of Alfred. Two were killed by deer hunters. I saw a very large one coming across a field, which crossed the road 20 feet ahead of my truck. Its speed really amazed me. No doubt in my mind now that a large coyote like I saw can pull a small deer on bare ground."

Among the more vociferous critics of the manner in which the Fisheries-Wildlife Department and its Research Unit has handled the coyote invasion are Herbert H. Foster of Orrington, formerly of Farmington, and Hal French of Wilton..

An octogenarian, Foster spent much of his life trapping and hunting in Maine. He has used the editorial pages of several newspapers and written articles assailing the "cuddling" of coyotes which he believes will eventually reduce the deer herd to where it may never again be restored. Having hunted bobcats with Foster I am fully aware of his powers of observation.

French has accumulated one of the largest files of fisheries and wildlife material in the country. He's been a long-time critic of what he describes as repeated research and frequently refers to it while appearing at legislative hearings.

"Final results of many projects are too often never made known," French contends, "and most of them are pigeon-holed to die with no benefit to fish and game."

French has continuously opposed research projects involving

coyotes in Maine on grounds they already have been completed in several other states.

"The scientific experts," French charges, "simply will not listen to anyone outside their realm. Typical example can be found in my home state of Maine where the experts refuse to accept or admit the inroads the northeastern coyotes have made on deer."

So anti-hunters and those who subscribe to the balance of nature theory will go on believing that the mongrel coyote is a welcomed addition to the state's wildlife, while the practical outdoors enthusiasts will continue to insist it is a threat to deer and could and should be controlled.

Thirty years ago deer could cope with hunting pressure, changes in habitat and predation mostly by bobcats. But with the tremendous increase in hunting pressure and the addition of a new and certainly more efficient predator, they have lost ground. Unless wildlife management in Maine changes its course and makes the welfare of the white-tailed deer a top priority, I am afraid that the future of this most valuable animal will remain in jeopardy.

Conclusion

I have felt like a voice in the wilderness and endured the harsh criticism of those who somehow view protection of the deer herd as a scheme to upset the delicate balance of nature. I also have enjoyed tremendous support — much of it from serious outdoorsmen — during my 20-year campaign to provide such protection by controlling the population of northeastern coyotes.

The vigil isn't over — it may, in fact, never end — but approval by the 111th Legislature of a limited predator-control program beginning in 1983 means the policymakers have at least begun to recognize the existence of a threat. And I no longer stand alone in my willingness to publicly express concern about the implications of the coyote menace. In fact, two of the state's most prominent wildlife experts — Carroll York and Fisheries-Wildlife Commissioner Glenn Manuel — agreed to outline their positions for this book.

York of West Forks, a veteran woods operator and keen observer, was the unanimous choice to head the Maine Deer Task Force recommended by the Sportsman's Alliance of Maine to evaluate the deer-coyote situation. Following is a summary of his findings:

"The coydog, as it was first called when it appeared in Maine, has become the most controversial animal that ever roamed our woods.

"The northeastern coyote, as it is now identified, first appeared in the early 1960s around the Spencer Lake-Enchanted areas and near West Forks. The first one I ever saw was killed by a pulp truck hauling on the Enchanted road.

"I have reports from reliable sources in Washington County that the animal seen there in the early 1960s was similar. This leads me to wonder whether this animal actually migrated into Maine, or is there a possibility that it was planted (stocked) by man in these areas?

"Whichever way the coyote came to Maine really does not matter. The sad truth is that it is now well established in all parts of the state. It is here to stay and is probably the most serious threat to Maine's wildlife, particularly deer, that we have known.

"From the time we first knew of the coyote's presence in the West Forks area to the 1970s, its numbers were not significant, but by the mid-1970s the animal apparently hit a peak population in this particular area and with this peak came the really severe drop in our deer herd.

"This drop occurred just as different other factors were having an adverse effect on deer, but there is no doubt in my mind that predation by the northeastern coyote was the major factor that caused the severe decline in deer numbers.

"It is now very obvious that the coyote spends most of his time in areas where there are a few deer. In my traveling from one area to another, I note that wherever I see deer tracks I also see coyote tracks and where there are no deer tracks coyote tracks are practically non-existent even though snowshoe hares may be plentiful.

"Should we make an attempt to eliminate the coyote from the woods of Maine? My answer would be no, as elimination is certainly not possible. But it is possible to control coyote numbers in Maine through trapping and every attempt should be made to do so.

"We had a week of ideal, warm trapping weather during the season of 1979 and coyote trapping success was so great in West Forks that there was a noticeable reduction of coyote tracks and signs the following winter.

"As to what the future will bring in regard to coyote populations and their effect on our deer herd, I do not believe anyone can accurately predict. But I feel sure that if the coyote remains at its present level and we do not make a very serious attempt to control its numbers, we are certainly jeopardizing any attempt to rebuild the deer herd in those parts of Maine where it has severely diminished."

Manuel became commissioner of the Inland Fisheries-Wildlife Department in 1979, succeeding Maynard F. Marsh.

Born in Hodgdon, Manuel's background has included many years of public service, much of it linked with the Fisheries-Wildlife Department. As a member of the state senate, he was chairman of the Legislative Committee on Fisheries and Game and headed the planning and interim study committees on Fisheries and Game.

Manuel was a member of the Advisory Council of the department from 1971 to 1977 and a member of the Waterfowl Advisory Council at the time of his appointment as commissioner.

Active in the potato industry, Manuel was president-owner of Potato Brokerage Firm of Presque Isle from 1967 to 1971 and either headed or served on several other major agricultural boards.

An experienced woodsman who came to the department when the coyote situation was a cause of major concern, Manuel's comments clearly indicate he has kept abreast of developments:

"Prior to the arrival of the early settlers in Maine, wolves covered the entire range of the State of Maine and successfully prevented the expansion of the white-tailed deer to the interior of the state. The only deer that existed in those days were along the coast or on coastal islands. Wolves being large aggressive animals, and hunting in packs prevented any expansion to interior Maine.

"As the settlers came, cleared the land, and moved inland and to the north, they successfully hunted the wolves and forced them to move north into Canada. As this movement took place, the deer began to thrive and move inland. Indeed they followed man from the length and breadth of the state. The early settlers had an expression that sums it up very well: 'The deer in Maine follow the axe.'

"From that period in history until about 15 to 20 years ago, predation from large canine animals upon other wildlife in Maine was practically non-existent. Foxes, fisher, bobcat, lynx and bear were the principal predators. In addition, there always has been a relatively insignificant number of wild dogs in Maine, who prey on wildlife.

"At this point I would like to point out that we are not talking about the well-known and established Western Coyote. Rather, we are talking about the so-called Eastern Coyote. Let's take a look at this new animal here in Maine. What is it? Where did it come from? What do we know about it?

"First, let me say that we got along very well without it from about 1700-1725 until about 15 or 20 years ago, and to quote former Commissioner Marsh (I fully agree) 'we don't need this animal in Maine and it is very unfortunate that we now have it. But have it we do, and we must learn to cope with it.'

"A lot has been written about its origin, but after sifting through the facts, there is no doubt in my mind that it is a combination of western coyote, wild dog, and wolf. They can and do interbreed, being of the canine family.

"These animals range in size from about 30 to 60 pounds when full grown, compared to 15 to 25 pounds for western coyote. Their conformation varies from the appearance of a German Shepherd-type dog to brush wolf to coyote. Their color ranges from light tan to dark brown and all sorts of combinations of the two.

"They have inherited the howl of a coyote, the pack-line hunting approach of the wolf, and are highly intelligent, which could be inherited from all three.

"These animals first became abundant in the western mountain regions near the Quebec border and expanded their range slowly in the beginning. During this period, the white-tailed deer was nearly wiped out in that area, and they still have not recovered despite hunting and trapping efforts on coyotes. Their predation was so thorough in many areas that no seed stock was left for regeneration.

"I should add that other factors also contributed to the demise of our most popular game animal, including bad cutting practices and unfavorable weather.

"As the food supply diminished, this animal did the natural thing and expanded its range, and within this 15 to 20 year period, they have covered most sections of the state. They, of course, eat daily therefore they hunt daily. They are especially damaging to our deer during deep snow periods in mid and late winter. We receive report after report of coyotes wiping out part or all of deer yards under certain circumstances. Deer, especially does heavy with fawn, are very vulnerable.

"I would like ... to lay aside the myth that coyotes take only the old and sick. Quite the contrary, they are indiscriminate but especially like does heavy with fawn. Many does are found dead, but only the unborn fawn is eaten.

"Their diet does not consist only of deer by any means. They, of course, eat berries, applies, nuts, grass, clover, etc.

"Deer are by no means the only animal they prey upon. They kill rabbit and beaver and are very competitive with other predators such as bobcat and fox, which they also kill.

"It is very difficult to determine how we are going to manage this animal along with our other wildlife in the future. But one thing is certain, if this animal is not kept in check, much of our other wildlife will suffer . . .

"If Maine sportsmen are to conserve and enhance their most sought after and prized animal, the white-tailed deer, they should unite and work with the Department of Inland Fisheries and Wildlife. Furthermore, they should work closely with the Maine Department of Agriculture and the U.S. Fish and Wildlife Service. Working together, progress can be made . . ."

Whatever happens, the threat to the Maine deer herd basically hasn't changed since the time I first reported it. The American public is quick to come to the defense of underdogs even when such a course might lead to national calamity. The sentiment is truer today than it was 20 years ago as far as predators are concerned. Continual efforts are made to have many of them, animals and birds, placed on the endangered list.

Lester McCann of the biology department of College of St. Thomas, St. Paul, Minn., warns against such a policy: "Let's not be afraid to tell sportsmen that they cannot expect prosperity for their game animals in a condition where the out-of-doors is dominated by the predatory animals."

McCann poses an important question in his highly controversial book *Time to Cry Wolf:* ". . . with overwhelming evidence that over-abundant predators are responsible for a general decline in wildlife numbers, why doesn't this translate into effective programs of predator control? This is even a greater mystery when you consider that increased predator numbers have been injurious to agricultural interests, also sapping the sheep industry to the tune of millions of dollars annually."

It has been especially difficult for me to reconcile the many articles, some in national magazines, which inaccurately report the northeastern coyote situation in Maine. As late as the winter of 1981 an article in Audubon magazine quoted Maine researchers as saying it had not been yet established that coyotes were killing deer or that some of the animals weighed more than 50 pounds. Unit researchers by then already had examined more than 40 deer kills by coyotes and a 78-pound coyote recorded as a Maine record.

One of the best examples of what a few northeastern coyotes can do to a herd of healthy whitetail deer occurred on Swan Island, off Richmond, Maine, from the fall of 1982 to the fawning period of 1983.

Robert Whitman was manager of this refuge during the period, retiring in October of 1983.

Swan Island lies in the Kennebec River at the head of Merrymeeting Bay, the state's major waterfowl concentration area. Channels flow by both the east and west shores, the former quite narrow, freezing over during the winter months.

Dedicated to Stephen Powell, a biologist with the Maine Department of Fisheries and Wildlife for many years, Swan Island is a haven for deer, being closed to hunting. During the winter the animals are fed regularly. Some commute to the mainland throughout the year.

According to the official record of the Fisheries-Wildlife department, on Dec. 25, 1982 one deer was observed down and injured on the ice between the island and Richmond Village by Whitman.

"Canine predation was assumed as the cause of mortality," the report read. "The incident was reported to Gary Donovan, the regional wildlife biologist.

From Jan. 1 to 20 ten deer carcasses were found and during this period coyotes "were believed to be the cause of mortality in the majority of the dead deer found."

Although five district wardens and John Hunt, small game furbearers project leader with the Department, were assigned in an effort to locate and catch coyotes, four of which were sighted Jan. 1 on the ice near the island, it was Feb. 11 before one was killed, shot by Whitman. It was a male weighing approximately 50 pounds.

I talked with Whitman several times about the situation. When the snow, which was less than average, disappeared and the ice on the river melted at least 30 deer were known to have been killed by the remaining coyotes.

Whitman described all the deer as "healthy animals" and of different ages. He told me the coyotes had destroyed a third of the known herd wintering on the island.

Whitman killed one more coyote. He sighted it as it was stalking a fawn. He could not give an estimate of the fawn losses from coyotes which took place from June until his retirement but felt sure several were killed by the predators.

This unfortunate loss of healthy, well fed deer, within 20 miles of the state capital, Augusta, created considerable discussion among Legislators and was partly responsible for the Committee on Fisheries and Wildlife earmarking an $85,000 appropriation for the new coyote control program.

The word bounty is anathema to scientific wildlife managers, yet the reduction of bobcat populations on two occasions has been linked directly to monetary incentive — higher bounties and a big hike in the raw fur market.

In Maine's severe climate, deer must have all the protection available if they are to maintain numbers that will provide reasonable hunting. The measures should include predator control that is sound, definite, organized and supervised.

There is a definite similarity in the attitude of most biologists toward any proposal to control populations of either the Brush Wolf or the northeastern coyote.

As this book was being printed they continued to insist neither animal has been or will be a serious threat to moose and deer populations, or to livestock.

The Minnesota Department of Natural Resources has sought for ten years — since Congress passed the Endangered Species Act — to regain management of the wolf population in that state. In 1978, the wolf status was downgraded from endangered to threatened allowing federal employees to trap and kill them. A court challenge by environmental and animal protection groups resulted in restrictions being imposed that allowed trapping only within one-quarter mile of farms where actual depredations had occurred.

L. David Mech, a U.S. Forest Service biologist, claims the present Minnesota control program has worked. Audubon magazine of March, 1983, quoted him as saying that wolves living directly beside farm pastures that were being radio-tracked did not once attack farm animals.

"It's as though they didn't recognize livestock as prey," Mech said. But the state of Minnesota continues to pay $400 a head for any livestock lost to wolves.

The Minnesota Department of Natural Resources has continued to insist that predator control is a matter of states rights and that it has personnel that can handle the problem.

The department's contention that the wolf is neither endangered and threatened and that it can stand a trapping and hunting season brings the wrath of environmental groups.

The latest verdict on the northeastern coyote or Brush Wolf control problem in Vermont is that "nothing is being done about it."

Biologist James DiStefano, in a release by the Vermont Fish and Game Department, says "predator control is only effective when efforts are directed at the offending animals only, not state-wide efforts."

This is a much quoted statement by the scientific divisions of all Fish-Game departments.

While Vermont's department spokesman says it is "almost universally agreed that there is a viable population of coyotes in Vermont. One of the most vocal concerns comes from deer hunters."

But, the spokesman continues, the size of the Vermont deer herd today is much lower than it was during the 1960s and 1970s. However, one of the management objectives of the department is to have a smaller deer herd so that food in areas where deer winter will improve resulting in fewer deer starving and a healthier deer herd.

There is evidence, the spokesman adds, that coyotes, like bobcat, prey on deer. However, research by the Vermont Fish-Game Department personnel and their colleagues in Maine and New York produces similar findings that coyotes are opportunist, feeding on anything that is seasonally available.

The spokesman added that biologists and wardens found less than one percent of the known deer deaths in that state in 1981 were caused by coyotes.

(Deer constituted over 30 percent of the diet of coyotes examined in Maine during a research project even when the animals examined were taken in late summer and fall months.)

The current coyote management program of the Vermont Fish and Game Department, however, now consists of:

Monitor population status through mandatory fur dealer reports and field staff observations;

Maintain current coyote trapping season and encourage coyote hunting;

Monitor sheep predation through field investigations and continue efforts to upgrade investigative skills of wardens and biologists;

Intensify cooperative programs with the Vermont Trappers Association to direct localized control efforts on offending coyotes and promote effective sheep husbandry as a countermeasure to predation through the state extension offices and Vermont Sheep Breeders Association.

The New Hampshire Fish and Game Department's attitude toward coyotes and their control is strikingly similar to that of the scientific division of the Maine department.

Despite the fact that a new coyote control program has been launched in which the University of Maine-Orono Wildlife Research unit will be excluded, Dr. James Sherburne, former head of the unit, remains adamant in his earlier evaluation of deer-coyote relations.

"The deer population (in Maine) is not in any danger, imme-

Dr. James Sherburne, leader of the University of Maine—Orono Wildlife Research unit. He was transferred to Africa in 1982.

diate or long range, from coyotes," Sherburne said in a unit release August 10, 1981. As far as I can ascertain he still hasn't changed his opinion.

Meanwhile, research projects on fur-bearers, including coyotes, costing $160,000 a year, have been continuing for four years under Sherburne and while due to expire in mid-1983 most likely will continue indefinitely.

At this writing, 71 coyotes had been radio-collared in these projects for what biologists describe as accurate tracking. Many sportsmen, whose taxes on various outdoor gear pay for such research, wonder why coyote control agents are not led to dens by such tracking when the Interior Department already is aware that finding such locations and eliminating dams and young are the most effective means of controlling populations of this predator.

FIELD SIGHTINGS AND NOTES

FIELD SIGHTINGS AND NOTES

FIELD SIGHTINGS AND NOTES